MONDO
LUCHA
A GO  GO

MONDO LUCHA A GO·GO

THE BIZARRE AND HONORABLE WORLD OF WILD MEXICAN WRESTLING

DAN MADIGAN

rayo *An Imprint of HarperCollinsPublishers*

HarperCollins books may be purchased for educational, business,
or sales promotional use. For information, please write: Special Markets Department,
HarperCollins Publishers Inc., 10 East 53rd Street, New York, NY 10022.

FIRST EDITION

Grateful acknowledgment is made for permissions for original photography from Edward
McGinty, Dorothy Lee, and David Chavira, copyright © 2007.

Designed by Renato Stanisic

Library of Congress Cataloging-in-Publication Data has been applied for.

ISBN: 978-0-06-085583-3

07 08 09 10 11 ❖/TOP 10 9 8 7 6 5 4 3 2 1

RIP

This book is dedicated to Eddie Guerrero...
a friend and champion.

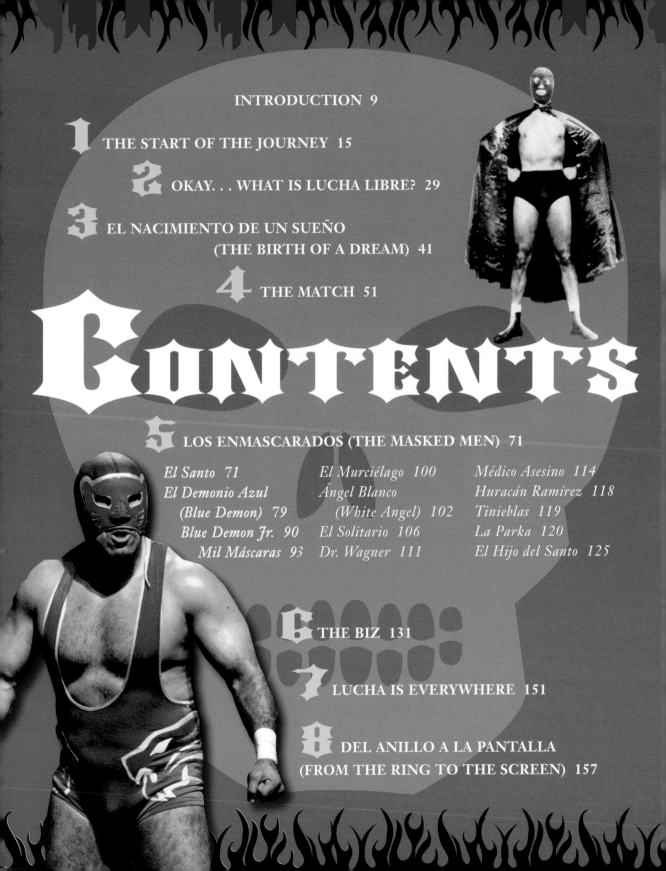

CONTENTS

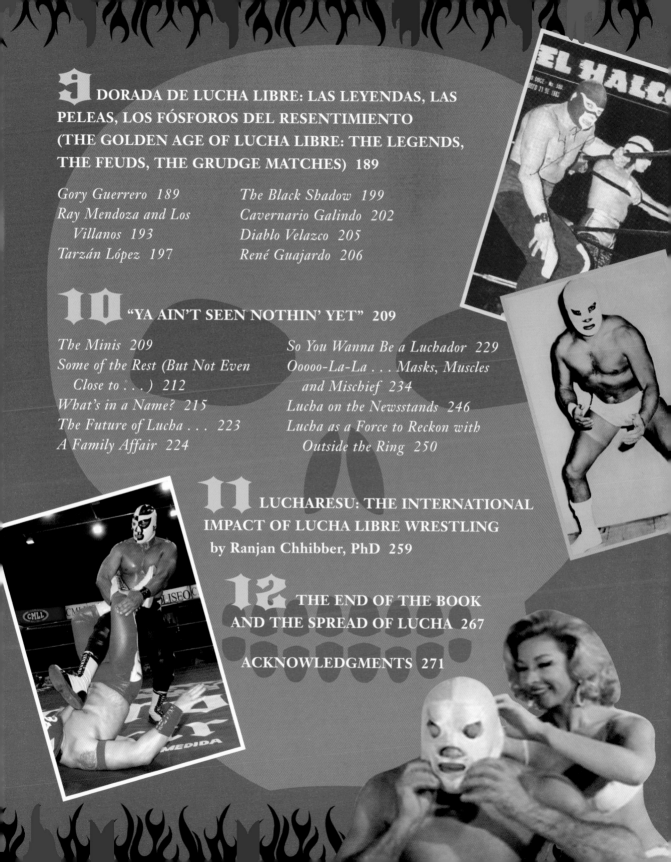

INTRODUCTION

LUCHA LIBRE—— *What can I say? Growing up in Pittsburgh, I didn't now what Lucha Libre was. All my time was spent on the mat or in the gym. My world of wrestling was confined first to the Mount Lebanon High locker room and then to the Tippin Gym at Clarion University. International competition took me to places all over the world and culminated in my gold medal victory in the 1996 Olympics in Atlanta in Freestyle Wrestling. I had been all over the planet, but the world of Lucha Libre had eluded me; at no time did I find myself in Mexico, or any other country that showcased it.*

I entered the ranks of pro wrestling in 1999 and have worked with some of the best athletes in the business. Tough, hard, talented, crazy men who are at the top of our profession. Two of the men that I have wrestled against— and with—are Rey Mysterio Jr. and Eddie Guerrero.

LEFT: *Miniestrella* **superstar Tsuki**

It was through Rey and Eddie that I started to learn what Lucha Libre was all about; both of them came from long, proud family lines that have been instrumental in the growth of the sport. Rey's uncle, Rey Misterio Sr., is a Lucha superstar who trained his nephew; Eddie's family, simply put, is legendary.

Wrestling against Rey Mysterio Jr. is like trying to catch a colorful ghost. His speed and talent were something I had never come across in the ring. Rey's moves were literally gravity-defying. His innate prowess, coupled with his Lucha training, have made Rey one of the most charismatic and tough wrestlers in the world today. Rey may not be as big as some of the other wrestlers I have challenged, but what he lacks in physical stature he more than makes up for with his heart and will.

BELOW: The quiet before the storm

As for Eddie, I don't know where to begin and I wouldn't know where to stop. I'll make it simple. Eddie Guerrero was one of the greatest wrestlers I have ever encountered. Anywhere. Period. What Eddie brought to the ring is something rare in our business: He was a superstar between the ropes and a leader behind the scenes. My matches against Eddie were brutal, and our feuds made me a better wrestler. My friendship with Eddie made me a better person. Eddie brought me to another level inside myself I never thought I had; he pushed me to brink and then knocked me over it. And it was there that I found out what I really was made of, not just as a wrestler but also as a human being. His untimely passing was a loss to our business and to this world that has left a lonely void that will never be filled.

And what was it that made these two become incredible and talented wrestlers, as well as honest, decent men? Lucha Libre. Lucha gave them two things that set them apart from others—heart and character. Many nights, Rey and Eddie wrestled in a lot of pain. Trust me, I know what it is like to walk out from behind the curtains in excruciating pain. I know what it feels like to get body-slammed when you have a pulled muscle or a torn hamstring. Pain is a constant companion in our business; it walks into the ring with you ever time you step between the ropes. Neither Rey nor Eddie ever complained or gave less than a hundred percent, no matter how much they hurt going into a match. Professionals, through and through.

And if Rey and Eddie are any indication of what type of men wrestle in the ranks of Lucha, all I have to say is this—thank God I am not working in Mexico! I don't know how I could face that type of talent and skill and tenacity night after night. Lucha was a part of the business I once knew nothing about; it is now a world I respect and admire. I have nothing but the utmost esteem for my Mexican counterparts and their traditions.

Rey, my friend, I wish you nothing but good health and the continued success you truly deserve. You are a champion with the heart of a lion. Eddie, my brother, may God hold you warmly in his arms until I see you again. Your brother, Kurt.

—Kurt Angle, Olympic Gold Medalist and Six-time WWE World Heavyweight Champion

Author's Note:

Kurt Angle won his Olympic gold medal with a broken neck! In the gold medal match, he also had two cracked vertebrae and two herniated discs. When a man like this speaks about character, he knows what he's talking about.

"MAN, EVIL IS REAL,

it is out there. Evil has a face, a look of its own and nothing else in the world looks like it. But for it to be truly terrifying, for evil to do its job it has to hide behind the mask. Evil has to function in society, it has to rub elbows with all the good folks and decent people, it has to be seen smiling all the time as it lurks and lives and breathes its fetid breath down our throats everyday. We live with the horror that, at any moment, at any time, that mask will slip off the person next to us and we'll see the face of true evil, true horror. So we ponder, bide our time, waiting for the mask of evil to fall off the faces of our neighbors, friends, co-workers and most of all ourselves. We wait to get a glimpse of what is behind the mask, to see what the face of evil really is, and when we see that true countenance of malevolence is that cold bland reflection we see in the mirrors every day, we know that the masks we all wear are one and the same. The monster does not need to hide his face, for his nature does not dictate shame or sin; it is man who must hide his true emotions and thoughts away from the world, lock them behind the facade, for truly there are no monsters like the ones that wear the human face."

—Tobe Hooper, Director of the original
Texas Chainsaw Massacre, *Salem's Lot*, and *Poltergeist*

I

> "God has given you one face, and
> you make yourself another."
> —William Shakespeare

The Start of the Journey

GOOD VERSUS EVIL *is one the oldest stories
in the world. It is basis of all dramatic storytelling from Greek
mythology to the Bible, from ancient legends to modern movies,
from comic books to pulp novels. Good versus evil is the main
event, the final showdown.*

    *Two rival gunslingers squaring off on
a dusty western town at high noon, ready
to blaze into American folklore. A pair
of Japanese samurais standing poised
with swords drawn, blades gleaming
in the setting sun in cherry blossom
orchard, ready to die to defend their
honor. Every culture has their heroes,
their villains, their stories, their mythos and legends.*

**OPPOSITE: Santo in the flesh: man, movie star, myth RIGHT: Even vampires aren't safe
from the Man in the Silver Mask**

In Latino culture, these stories are played out within the squared circle—all the passion, pageantry, emotion, violence, adventure, love and hate find their outlet in the ropes of the wrestling ring. They call it Lucha Libre and that name resonates respect and awe throughout the Latin world. A combination of sport, entertainment and dramatic storytelling all rolled up into one flamboyant display. Lucha Libre can be realistic combat or over the top, wild and high-flying insanity. It's an infectious way of life, a crowd-screaming spectacle and just plain fun.

I remember the first time I saw him on the screen of my grandfather's black-and-white television. The local UFH station flickered snowy images, and at times the reception was so bad that phantom images wavered across the screen. The picture vacillated between slightly discernible

BELOW: When Santo made his way to American airwaves in the '60s, he went by the name Samson

FILMADORA PANAMERICANA, S. A. presenta :

SANTO EL ENMASCARADO DE PLATA

LORENA VELAZQUEZ · JAIME FERNANDEZ
MARIA DUVAL · AUGUSTO BENEDICO
Y LA ACTUACION ESTELAR DE

OFELIA MONTESCO

SANTO VS. LAS MUJERES VAMPIRO

con XAVIER LOYA · FERNANDO OSES · LOBO NEGRO · FRANKENSTEIN · CAVERNARIO GALINDO · RAY MENDOZA · BLACK SHADOW
BOBY BONALES · EDUARDO BONADA

Argumento ANTONIO ORELLANA · FERNANDO OSES · RAFAEL GARCIA · TRAVESI Adaptacion R. GARCIA TRAVESI

ABOVE: One of the all-time Santo classics, loaded with some of the greatest names in Lucha Libre

to out of focus . . . but
he stood there in all of his static-infused glory,
the most unique person I had ever seen, El Santo. Legend, myth and
hero. A silver-masked man who flew around the ring like a dervish,
all high-flying moves and devastating punches and kicks.

    I had seen American wrestling on Saturday mornings. I was an
avid reader of comic books and a fanatical fan of horror movies, but
for the first time everything I loved was rolled into one big mass of
righteous Mexican muscle under a mysterious silver mask. Nothing
I had seen up to that point was as awe-inspiring as the image of El
Santo. The audio was badly dubbed and I couldn't follow the story,
but from that moment I was hooked. But there was a problem. My
chance encounter with El Santo was something of a fluke. I didn't
know who El Santo was at the time, or how to find out anything

PELÍCULAS Rodrigues S.A. Presenta a:

Episodios:

"LA MAFIA"

"MUERTE EN EL FRONTON"

FERNANDO

SANT

SANOVA • ANA BERTHA LEPE en

CON SANTO

O CONTRA EL REY DEL CRIMEN

"EL ENMASCARADO DE PLATA"

BETO EL BOTICARIO • RENE CARDON•
AUGUSTO BENEDICO • ANTONIO RAXE•
GUILLERMO ALVARES BIANCHI
YOLANDA CIANI.
Actuaciones especiales

about him, or if that station would ever play another Santo film. I can't even remember the title of the film I saw him in that day, but his image was burned into my mind, and my imagination was raging full-blown Lucha Libre before I even knew what Lucha Libre was.

Cut to several years later. I'm an anxious adolescent looking through some secondhand wrestling magazines in a comic-bookshop. I come upon a battered issue of *Pro Wrestling Illustrated* magazine, and on the cover I see that face I remembered so vividly staring out at me from the creased and torn cover. El Santo . . . WOW! That same feeling of excitement I felt years earlier came rushing back. I grabbed the magazine without even looking through it, threw my seventy-five cents on the counter and ran outside.

To a kid growing up in the United States, Mexico might as well have been another planet. It was wildly different from anything I ever knew in the Boston area of the seventies. Mexico was a land of intrigue, a country of mystery. These masked men were walking, talking, flying, fighting superheroes and I thought the Mexican people were lucky to have them living among them. Instead of existing only on the pages of a comic book, these masked heroes or *enmascarados* (masked wrestlers) came to life in the middle of the ring. I had to find out more about El Santo and the rest of the wrestlers known as Luchadores who lived south of the border.

What little information I gathered about El Santo, Mil Máscaras and other Luchadores was from the wrestling commentators on Saturday morning who would call Mil Máscaras matches and talk about the colorful details of the Luchadores' careers. Occasionally American wrestling magazines would run articles about the Luchadores and cover something in the Lucha Libre world, but that wasn't enough for me.

The journey that started when I saw my first masked Luchador years earlier on my grandfather's TV had now grown into a full-blown quest. I spent so much money on a

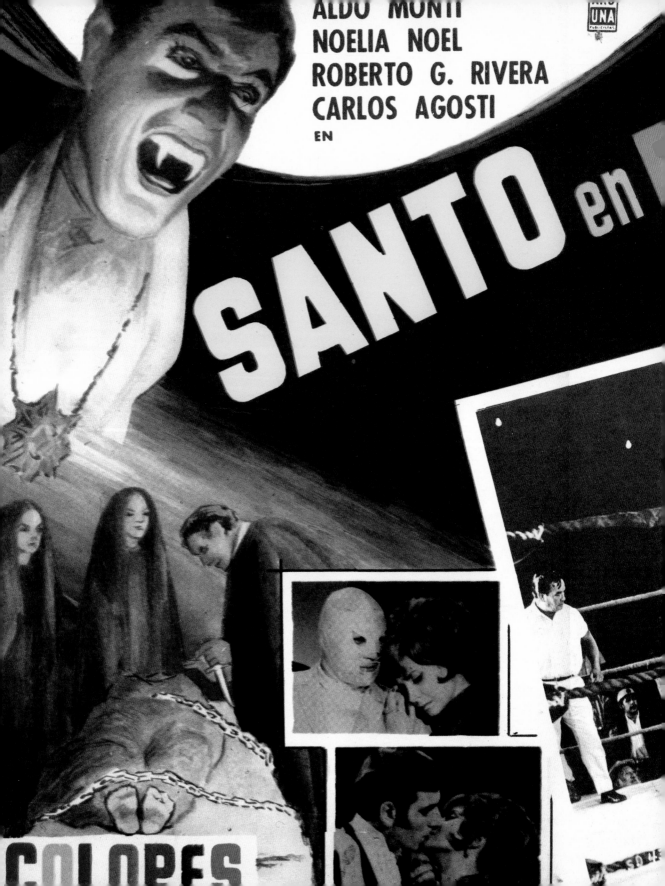

EL TESORO DE DRÁCULA

con
ALBERTO ROJAS y
la niña **PILI GONZALEZ**

Filmica VERGARA (CINECOMISIONES, S.A.) presenta a SANTO EL ENMASCARADO DE PLATA EM:

PROFANADORES DE TUMBAS

"LOS TRAFICANTES DE LA MUERTE"

GINA ROMAND · MARIO OREA · JORGE PERAL
JESSICA MUNGUIA · JESUS CAMACHO

Con

FERNANDO OSES
LOBO NEGRO
BIGOTON CASTRO
JORGE FEGAN
FERNANDO SAUCEDO

PRODUCCION
LUIS ENRIQUE
VERGARA CABRERA

Dirección y Guión Técnico   Argumento y Adaptación   Fotografía
JOSE DIAZ MORALES   RAFAEL GARCIA TRAVESI EDUARDO VALDEZ

PT-126

ABOVE: The art on these lobby cards accentuates the story, unlike American posters today that are usually boring images of overpriced stars

succession of badly dubbed, poorly recorded, fourth-generation bootleg El Santo videos that came out of Mexico in the eighties. Half the time the action on the screen was so dark I wondered if the television was even on. Most movies looked like they were filmed at night in some arena where lighting hadn't even been invented yet. The atrocious audio didn't matter because they were speaking Spanish anyway, and subtitles weren't even a consideration.

But it didn't matter to me. El Santo was on the screen, wrestling opponents in the ring and battling monsters, mummies, vampire women and other assorted supernatural villains outside of it. He was my Latin Batman, my Mexican Superman, and he could do no wrong. It was at this time that I came to know Mexican cinema—or what

I thought Mexican cinema to be—movies with wrestling, fighting monsters, more wrestling, men in masks and more wrestling thrown in for good measure. A discerning film critic I was not.

The top three stars of Lucha Libre filmdom were (are and always will be) El Santo, Mil Máscaras, and Blue Demon. These three Luchadores starred in over a hundred movies combined. Now, not every movie was a classic. These films varied in quality from good to fair to bad to "I can't believe I just spent twenty-two fifty on this." But when you're a fan, you don't mind shelling out the bucks because that's what fans do—we watch, we track down, we collect because we are obsessed.

It could be said that El Santo, Blue Demon and Mil Máscaras are just as important to Mexican artistic culture as the famed trio of muralists,

BELOW: Two superstars for the price of one: Santo and Blue Demon battle the evil Dr. Frankenstein

EL CREADOR DE MONSTRUOS Y CADAVERES VIVIENTES DE BELLAS MUJERES, SE ENFRENTA A LOS DEFENSORES DE LA JUSTICIA.

SANTO y BLUE DEMON CONTRA EL DR. FRANKESTEIN

SANTO · BLUE DEMON
EL ENMASCARADO DE PLATA
SASHA MONTENEGRO · JORGE RUSSEK · IVONNE GOVEA

ABOVE: Supreme gives body, soul, and blood at an FCW show in Inglewood

Diego Rivera, David Alfaro Siqueiros, and Jose Orozco. Instead of walls and buildings, the Luchadores' canvases are the wrestling rings and movie screens, their mission statements just as important as their artistic counterparts', their goals just as noble and politically minded. Good is triumphant over evil, light vanquishes darkness, justice prevails. Every kick, leap and punch was a brush stroke in the masterpiece of storytelling they created. The Luchadores are larger than life yet real and tangible. Everyday heroes who walk the streets with their masks on and yet don't seem out of place; they inhabit a world that embraces the fantastic and bizarre.

But the history and legacy of Lucha Libre is not confined to the exploits and adventures of these three Luchadores. It has a rich history that predates El Santo and flourishes today. And, to my surprise, not every wrestler wears a mask. Many a man has braved entrance into the ring with his face and identity exposed to the world. Many Luchadores preferred their real names and faces be shown for the world to clearly see. Legendary names like Gory Guerrero and the Guerrero family, Ray Mendoza, Perro Aguayo and many others wrestled for decades without a mask.

And Lucha Libre isn't confined exclusively to the Mexican culture. Its roots are in Mexico, but Latin wrestlers from Puerto Rico, Cuba, South America, the Caribbean and even Japan have embraced and been influenced by the incredible Lucha Libre style. After almost eighty years Lucha Libre is gaining unprecedented popularity.

An American Kid on His Way to Becoming a Lucha Fan

Wrestling has endured on television for over half a century. When TV started to make its appearance in homes throughout the country in the 1950s, one of the first staples was professional wrestling. Television and pro wrestling were made for each other; they go hand in hand in entertaining the masses.

Like many guys of my age, I was smitten by professional wrestling, it was unbelievably important to my friends and me. I cannot tell you how many times my pals and I would copy the wrestling moves we saw on television. Rather poorly, of course, and our bruises and black eyes were painful reminders of our youthful ineptitude. Being born and raised in Boston, the only wrestling I was exposed to was the old WWWF that dominated the Northeast. All I knew growing up was the spectacular "Superstar" Billy Graham, Andre the Giant, King Kong Bundy, Hulk Hogan, etc.—the list of men of girth and volatile tempers is too long to list. But in the '70s, coming out of the south from Mexico was Mil Máscaras. I had seen El Santo before on that hard-to-see UHF station, but seeing a masked wrestler work in the ring was a real treat. There had been others, but none possessed the appeal and intrigue Mil Máscaras had at the time. Where did this guy come from? What did he look like under the mask? Could he pick up girls with that thing on? And if he did, how could I get my hands on one?

> "Man is least himself when he talks in his own person. Give him a mask, and he will tell you the truth."
> —Oscar Wilde

Okay . . . What Is Lucha Libre?

IF YOU HAVE investigated the inside of this book, you probably have a pretty good idea what Lucha Libre is, and if you are a fan, there is no need to tell you. But what is Lucha Libre exactly? The term itself means "free-style fighting." What is "free-style fighting"? It is a combination of various fighting techniques: wrestling, judo, jujitsu, grappling, kickboxing and boxing. It is the mixture

of all these combative art forms blended with the elements of soap opera and dramatic storytelling, physical comedy, incredible athletics, suspense and intrigue.

As North America, Mexico, and Japan all have their own distinct styles, what separates Mexican wrestling from its American,

OPPOSITE: The high-flying Místico sails into a Flying Head Scissors ABOVE: Banner for Rocky Roman's FMLL monthly Lucha Libre shows in Compton, California

Canadian or Japanese counterparts? It's the action. The in-ring action of a Lucha Libre match has to be seen to be believed. I can write about it, turn a few colorful phrases, but nothing really delivers the impact like being there. These wrestlers, Luchadores—athletes, acrobats, performers—put on a nightly show of unbridled energy and contagious, enthusiastic showmanship. Lucha Libre is over the top—there is no better way to try to describe it.

I am not going to get into the discussion question that plagues wrestling fans from the people who balk at their passion, "Well, is it *real?*" It is real enough. The wrestlers connect with their fans in a way that is almost familial. I had never seen a real-life Lucha Libre match until not too long ago. I had considered myself a fan but how much of a fan could I have been if I had not gone to the small venues to watch the shows that were plentiful around Los Angeles?

One night I was at dinner with some friends, telling them about the Lucha Libre book I was planning to write. I mentioned I was going down to Compton to cover a Lucha event. The table went dead silent. I looked up from shoveling food into my mouth to see that the couple hosting our dinner were both looking at me like I had two heads. I tried to calculate whatever type of social faux pas I may have made (which I am legendary for doing, at the wrong place and wrong time). "You're going to Compton?" they both said in curious unison. "Yeah." I shrugged. "You better bring a gun," the husband told me. Now it was my turn to be incredulous. "What did you say?" I blurted out.

Where did they think I was going? Downtown Baghdad? Fallujah wearing an Uncle Sam costume? I don't even own a gun and even if I did I sure as hell wouldn't be

BELOW: One of the great Lucha Libre magazines, *El Halcon,* signed by the cowardly El Cobarde II himself

ABOVE: This magnicent pencil drawing of Santo was commissioned especially for this book by noted artist Antonio Pelayo

bringing it anywhere with me. I laughed it off. Their concern was genuine but unfounded. Granted, there are parts of Compton that I, a middle-aged white man, would not venture into, but there are places in most major cities I would not travel. This was the first taste of the misgivings I would encounter on my journey trying to write this book. Preconceptions about people, places and cultures abounded.

My first stop was a city that isn't known by the outside world as a Lucha Libre stronghold—Compton, a place whose reputation precedes it. I went down on a sunny Sunday afternoon. I was traveling with my photographer Ed and my friend Antonio, who was going as my interpreter. As I began searching for the local Lucha Libre scene

LEFT: Setting up an Off the Top Rope Suplex: very effective and very dangerous for both men involved

ABOVE: The Blue Panther purrs prior to pouncing

in Los Angeles I came upon a handbill in front of a newsstand that announced some matches in Compton. It seemed like a godsend: I was at this particular newsstand to look for any magazine that could lead me in the right direction and I found a piece of paper with the time and location. Perfect. We drove down the 110 and found the hall with the big bright sign that read FMLL (La Fuerza Mexicana de Lucha Libre) that was founded in 1999 by Rocky Roman and is one of the better-run promotions around.

Ed was going over his cameras and preparing his equipment as Antonio and I, anxious and excited, headed into the building. At first I thought all the eyes looking in my direction were nothing more than middle class paranoia but then the ticket guy looked up at me with wide eyes. So did the kid sitting next to him handing out flyers for the next show. I headed inside, and it felt like one of those scenes out of an old Western movie when the stranger walks into the saloon and all eyes turn to look at him. I was that stranger. I was the outsider trying to look in.

Antonio whispered to me, "Man, they are all checking you out." I looked around and realized I was the only non-Hispanic in the room.

"I'm the only gringo here. That's why," I told him.

"No, man. They think you are a wrestler!" he said. Then it hit me: They did think I was a wrestler. The fact that I had been a grappler and wrestler and that I am a former powerlifter who walks around with some girth (too much girth, if you ask some people) caused everyone staring to mistake me for one of the guys who should have been in the ring.

It struck me how funny it was that the first thing that came to my mind was that I was being scrutinized because of my race, when in reality I was being looked over because the fans thought I was a Luchador. Another misconception and it was on my part. I looked around the place for Rocky Roman. He is the promoter and founder of FMLL and I found his number on the flyer. After I spoke to Rocky on the phone and told him who I was and what I was doing, he invited me down to his show. As I searched the crowd I saw a guy standing at a table supervising the sale of some souvenir masks of some of the more popular wrestlers. He looked up and I could tell that this was Rocky. He is a thin man with an infectious broad smile. We shook hands and he told me he would answer any questions I had about Lucha Libre. He founded FMLL in 1999 and since then has had some great performers and fantastic cards at his venue. Then it hit me: what exactly did I want to ask?

Like all wrestling or boxing events, you start the card with the lesser-known talents. In American wrestling they are called "dark matches" and in boxing they still go by the term "prelims." These first few matches are haphazard and very raw, and the wrestlers, who for the most part are not wearing masks, go back and forth with only a few standard moves. Of course that doesn't matter to the crowd. There is a hero to cheer and a villain to jeer and a story to tell within the ropes. That is why they are there, that is why they come down with their kids, wives, grandparents to continue the weekly ritual that was started a long time ago in a far-off place. The action that was going on in the ring was just as fascinating as the action going on in the stands. There is nothing quite like the fans at a Lucha Libre event. I have been to American football, baseball, hockey, basketball games all of it, and even though some of those attendance numbers dwarf the small Lucha venues, the intensity and passion generated through those little bingo halls or back rooms is enough to power a whole stadium.

BELOW: *Miniestrella* superstar Tsuki heads to the ring: the power of an atomic bomb packed into a firecracker

I turned to Antonio and asked him who his favorite Mexican wrestler was. He looked at me and smiled and said, "Santo . . . of course."

"When did you first see a Santo match?" I asked. His response intrigued me.

"I never saw Santo wrestle. I was very little when he passed away and if I did see him wrestle I don't remember."

"How can a guy you may or may not have seen perform be your favorite wrestler?" His answer summed it all up.

"Man, it's SANTO!"

That was it. Most of today's Lucha fans never saw the original Santo wrestle (they may have seen his son and cheered him on). But a man who has been dead for over ten years and retired from the ring longer still resonated as the perennial crowd favorite. What was it that made this guy so popular? What was it that put El Santo in a state of natural veneration in Mexico? You don't have to be Mexican or Latino to understand but it does help. To some, Santo is as much a figure in Mexican history as Zapata or the Virgin of Guadalupe, and in some households exalted to that level of sainthood that his name implies. But how? Come on. It's just wrestling . . . or is it?

BELOW: Even under his mask, Dr. Wagner Jr.'s disdain for his opponents is clearly visible

Wrestling fans are tremendously passionate people. Try sitting next to some during a match. I've seen grandmothers actually smash wrestlers across their heads with purses as the Luchadores fell from the ring and into the seats where we were sitting. As clichéd as that image is, it was true. I've seen people toss their beers at the bad guys (uncool), and I've seen bad guys getting hit with beer and pretending to like the taste (very cool). I've heard old women and young children blurt out a litany of Spanish indecencies that sounded like one continuous, boisterous howl. What is it that makes people so crazed and emotional about athletic competition? Is it the fact that most people can't compete so they put their hopes, dreams, and desires into the ones who can? So that when fans cheer on their heroes, they are cheering on that part of themselves? Do Luchadores wrestle by emotional proxy for all of us?

And when we boo the villain, are we chastising the dark side that is in all of us, the side we know is there but try to keep pushed back? No other sport in the world has these dualistic elements like wrestling. Even boxing doesn't have the same heroic and villainous roles. But why is wrestling so emotionally draining for the spectators as well as the competitors? Is it because of the arousing nature of physical confrontation? Wrestling is without a doubt the toughest sport in the world. There is nothing easy about another guy trained to beat you into submission. Most other aggressive sports, boxing and weightlifting aside, are team competition. In wrestling it is one on one, even in tag team competition. "Officially" it is only man against man at any given time, but wrestling is a sport where any weakness will be exploited immediately.

"The origins of the word *mask* are unclear, but it probably comes from the Arabic *maskhara* (*mashara*), which meant 'to falsify' or 'transform' into animal, monster, or freak."
—from *Masks: Faces of Culture* by John W. Nunley and Cara McCarty

Wrestling has been around as long as man has been on this planet. The oldest sport in the world was the combative struggle between two competitors, the loser sometimes forfeiting his life. Every culture and society has had some form of wrestling, or its people have practiced their grappling skills. In ancient Egypt, wrestlers first appear in the Old Kingdom tomb of Ptahhotep (2300 B.C.). The Greeks had the art of Pankration. Tribes of the Far and Middle East, American Indians, the peoples of Asia, and peoples all throughout the world have always regard wrestling as one of the most brutal sports to endure.

American professional wrestling grew from the carny sideshows of the early part of the last century. Back then, the carnival circuit ran the gamut from clean and friendly fairs with rides and honest games of chance to sideshows that were filled with freaks, oddities, scantily clad women, and dishonest barkers.

Puritanical leanings aside, the carny circuit was a place where the local townsfolk came to spend some money, eat some candy and see another side of life they didn't get the opportunity to experience in their suburban lives. A major part of the carny shows was the circus strongman. These legendary men of strength, from Eugen Sandow, "Father of Modern Bodybuilding," to Louis Cyr, have all, at one time or another, been part of the carnival circuit. The other manly aspect was the wrestling or "wrassilin' " exhibitions that were put on between carny ringers and the local gentry. There, in those simple and friendly (but rough) competitions, the seeds of an industry were planted.

Within a few years these "grappling" matches became the showcase event of many carnivals. Their popularity grew, and in the late twenties and thirties professional wrestling was being promoted in the same venues as prizefighting. By "professional wrestling," I mean the type of wrestling that most Americans were familiar with at the time. Amateur wrestling, the hard sport of Greco-Roman, and free-style wrestling, did not have the flair or dramatics that "pro" wrestling has, which is unfortunate because amateur (or collegiate) wrestling is one of the most challenging sports to compete in.

At the same time pro wrestling was hitting its first zenith in America, it began to flourish in Europe as well. The one country that readily adopted the competitive nature and dramatic flair that professional wrestling carried was Spain. The Spanish wholeheartedly accepted the entire machismo concept—fighting for honor. The Spanish style of wrestling was heavily influenced by what was called "catch as catch can" in America. "Catch as catch can" (shortened to "catch") began in the late 1800s in the United States when old-time traveling carnival circuits traveled about, staging "athletic shows," or friendly grappling matches, and money wagers between the performers and the locals.

It was this fast-paced, hard style of wrestling that the Spanish learned and taught to their Mexican counterparts. The "catch" style gradually morphed into the Lucha Libre style. There was a harmonious union between Mexico and Spain when it came to sharing wrestling ideologies, training techniques and styles until the

Spanish Civil War put the kibosh on Mexican wrestlers going to Spain to practice their craft. The Corporacion Internacional de Catch ran wrestling in Spain. This corporation based its blueprint on boxing, using different weight classes (not to mention incorporating some of the more shady and dishonest ways of doing business that had plagued boxing for years). When the war heated up in Spain, many of the top wrestlers, trainers and promoters moved to Mexico. Spain's loss was Mexico's gain, and the influx of these expatriates improved the quality of its matches and management, organization and promotion. Lucha Libre now had the foundation to grow into something great. After the war, Lucha returned to Spain, but by the early 1960s the public had lost interest in the sport that, years before, had seemed poised to rival soccer as the favorite Spanish pastime.

Wrestling is always unique to the country in which it's located, but merging styles would be part of the Lucha Libre tradition. Like the ultimate fighters of today, who cross-train in several styles, the Luchadores cross-train so they can compete against anything they may face.

The Lucha Libre phenomenon in Mexico began in the early 1930s. In a small town between Texas and Mexico a man with both hindsight and vision saw something unfold before his eyes, something that hit a chord deep inside of him. Something that would resonate with his people for years to come.

ABOVE: Luchadores battle in a Sunday afternoon FMLL show with the feared and seldom used Toe to the Nose Lunge

3

El Nacimiento de un Sueño
(The Birth of a Dream)

AT LIBERTY HALL *in El Paso, Texas, in a crowded, hot, and sweaty building, Don Salvador Lutteroth, a successful businessman and entrepreneur, attended a wrestling match. Nothing out of the ordinary, nothing spectacular, just a humid night and a room packed with a throng of cheering, rabid wrestling fans. But the evening's entertainment triggered something in Lutteroth's imagination. It was there he first glimpsed an American masked wrestler named "Cyclone" McKey (often referred to as "Ciclón" McKey).*

It was a moment of great revelation. He saw the crowd's reaction. He heard the noise. He felt the energy of the night and the mystery surrounding the unknown grappler's aura in the ring.

LEFT: Enmascarado legends Blue Demon and El Santo, a teaming of mythic proportions ABOVE: The mind that started it all, Don Salvador Lutteroth

Knowing business and knowing his own people, he knew instantaneously that the addition of the masked wrestler to Mexican Lucha Libre was perfect to energize the sport. It was one of the most prophetic nights in wrestling history.

This creation myth is undisputed. It was Don Salvador Lutteroth who, after seeing a masked wrestler in Liberty Hall, Texas, knew that the people of Mexico would embrace and love this combination of sport, wrestling and entertainment. He was the Don King/Vince McMahon/P. T. Barnum/Walt Disney of Lucha Libre, a visionary who shaped, molded, and created a new, phenomenal style of wrestling: a form of entertainment and a source of national pride that exploded across Mexico and South America.

Born in 1897 in Colotlan, a small town in the western part of Mexico, Don Salvador Lutteroth's beginnings were humble. His family worked hard and wanted the best for the youngster. Still in his teens, Lutteroth enrolled in agricultural school in Mexico City, but due to the untimely death of his father, Lutteroth was forced to return home to help support his family. Job prospects were scarce then, political unrest was in the air, and people were uncertain about the government. Needing work, Lutteroth joined the Mexican army; it was an opportunity to get a steady paycheck and food in his stomach. Lutteroth had a natural drive that propelled him up the army ranks from foot soldier to first captain by 1923.

After he left the army he worked in the Mexican Tax Office. The job required a lot of travel, and Lutteroth frequently found himself on the road. In Texas he attended his first professional wrestling match. Realizing the future potential of that sport, he, along with his business partner Francisco Ahumada, combined a small number of backers to start the company Empresa Mexicana de la Lucha Libre, running shows in a decrepit building named Modelo Arena by 1933. A decade later, the first arena built exclusively for Lucha Libre broke ground—Arena Coliseo, a new building that was larger and designed especially for the growing number of Lucha fans.

Now Don Salvador Lutteroth's dream would have a permanent 3,000-seat arena to call its home. A natural-born showman and promoter, Lutteroth put on first-rate shows with the best Lucha Libre talent around. He imported wrestlers from around the world to come wrestle in Mexico. It was an international smorgasbord of talent, technique and styles to which the Mexican fans were treated. Shows consistently sold out and fans were turned away at the doors. This was during the Second World War, a time when money was tight, but no matter—people couldn't get enough.

Noted wrestlers like Bobby Sampson from the United States, "Ciclón" McKey, and the American Indian wrestler Yaqui Joe all came to wrestle under Lutteroth's banner. In a short time, small venues were popping up and hosting their own local Lucha events. Lucha became a sport that rivaled soccer for public attention and fanfare, and this is years before the sport had any television coverage. The popularity of Lucha Libre paid for itself; the Arena Coliseo was soon not big enough for the Lucha crowds. Lutteroth built an even bigger arena, the 20,000-seat Arena Mexico, in the heart of Mexico City, which opened its doors to tremendous public reaction in 1956.

LEFT: Los Hermanos Shadows: Black Shadow and Blue Demon

ABOVE: A trio of Lucha greats (l. to r.): Rayo de Jalisco, Black Shadow, and Santo

MASKS

"We all wear masks, and the time comes when we cannot remove them without removing some of our own skin."
—ANDRÉ BERTHIAUME, *CONTRETEMPS*

I assumed, like many Lucha fans, that the concept of masked wrestling must have naturally come from Mexico's rich past. The pre-Hispanic indigenous peoples of Mexico—Aztecs, Incas, Mayans, indeed all the indigenous peoples of South and Central America—used masks in their ceremonies and traditional dramas, including animal masks, and masks that depicted demons and heroes. The masked character would symbolize the spirit of the jungle or the personification of an enemy or invader. A performer wearing the mask of a ferocious beast—a snarling jaguar or leopard—became infused with those animals' qualities. Much like the Passion plays that swept through Europe, these passionate plays of masked men dressed as beasts, heroes, and villains enflamed the hearts of the people who came to watch and participate in them.

But the concept of the masked wrestler began as a North American gimmick. In 1915, when a wrestler named the "Masked Marvel" or, in Spanish, "La Maravilla Enmáscarada" (disguised wrestler Mort Henderson) first made his appearance in New York, the gimmick of a masked wrestler already existed. The contrivance originated when a wrestler began to lose popularity or had played through the territory so often that he wasn't bringing in the gate (returns at the box office). He might have started to work in other parts of the country where he was less known. The best way to work and keep one's identity a

BELOW: No pain

secret was to don a mask, take up a new moniker, and start a feud with a popular wrestler in another territory. It was business. If the wrestler didn't want to break his contract with the promoter, or if he had the promoter's blessing (and of course a percentage of the wrestler's purse), he could work in other territories without fear his original persona or real identity would be revealed.

When Lucha Libre began to catch on in Mexico in the thirties, there were no specialty stores a prospective wrestler could walk into in order to obtain a mask. You couldn't stroll into your local tailor and say, "Yes, I need something for my face. Make it tight-fitting to the point of painful, hard to breathe through, and almost impossible to see out of." Yet those were the specifications to which some of the earliest masks were constructed. Comfort and practicality were not priorities in the first *máscaras* (masks) for enmascarados.

Enter a humble shoemaker from Mexico City named Antonio H. Martínez, a transplant from Leon Guanajuato who moved to the capital in the 1920s. Martínez, a fan of Lucha Libre, was known for creating specialty wrestling boots for some of the Luchadores. One of Martínez's first customers was his favorite Luchador, Charro Aguayo. When Aguayo discovered that his number-one fan was a shoemaker he asked Martínez to design a boot for him.

Up until then Luchadores wore boxing shoes, and although these shoes were made to move easily around the ring, they did not give the ankle support needed by the Luchador.

Where boxers bob and weave, stalking their opponents and dancing around the ring, Luchadores fly across the ring; they dive, tumble, fall and crash onto the ropes (and, if outside, onto the hard concrete floor). The boot that Martínez developed for the Luchadores helped give extra ankle and arch support by absorbing the shock and lessening the impact on the body. The design of the heavy rubber-soled boot was made to personal specifications.

ABOVE: Once hidden behind the mask, a Luchador's true self comes out in the ring

It wasn't long after that Martínez became known as the go-to man for specialty in-ring attire that "Ciclón" McKey, who had been working in Mexico, went to Martínez and asked if he could make McKey a mask to wrestle in. The first prototypes consisted of two pieces of tough suede sewn together; the material was coarse, didn't allow much movement and made it nearly impossible to breathe—not very conducive to performing long, hot matches. But after going back to the sewing machine, Martínez came upon a design that is still in use today with modern materials.

Four pieces of material were sewn together to cover the entire head. There were openings for the mouth, eyes and nose. Around the exposed features were colors or some type of design and pattern to draw emphasis to the nose, eyes and mouth. The back of the mask was open, and had a tongue of the same material. There were laces so it could be tied up securely. Each enmascarado had his own measurements built into the design; it was not uncommon for enmascarados to travel from all parts of the country to visit Martínez's shop in Mexico City.

This design stayed constant for decades, but like every art form, derivation was to be expected. In the 1970s some enmascarados (El Solitario, for one) designed their máscaras to be opened in the lower jaw area. The mouth and jaw were exposed while the rest of the head (with the exception of the nose and eyes) was still covered by the material.

Jesús Velázquez was one of the first Mexicans to use a mask in the ring. He was known as El Murciélago (The Bat). He would enter the ring in a leather mask and cape, and in a stroke of showmanship brilliance, he would release a bag of live bats into the arena. You have to love the fact that not only did he *not* care about the commotion that live bats would cause in the rafter seats, he had no regard for the potential outbreak of rabies—that, *dear readers*, is showmanship extraordinaire.

The earliest masks were simple in their design and especially color; you had to be able to see the mask from the farthest seat away from the ring. Wrestlers had to choose what designs and colors best suited their personality in the ring. Today, mask making has become an art form. In the 1990s mask design became increasingly more creative. With wrestlers like

Psicosis, Juventud Guerrera and Rey Mysterio Jr., the colors became more garish (if possible), and fringe, horns, beaks, hair, feathers, and all types of protrusions and projections started to appear on the máscaras of the enmascarados. In many ways these new, wild, more elaborate designs harkened back to the pre-Hispanic masks used by the indigenous people of Mexico.

El Santo's former mask maker Ranuelfo López's family has kept the tradition of creating and designing masks for Luchadores alive for three generations now, and just as Santo passed on his mask to his son, Santo's mask maker passed on the tradition and honor of creating such sacred relics to his own children. One of the top mask makers in Los Angeles is Juan Guerrero. He runs a nice little shop in San Gabriel and local enmascarados as well as wrestlers from Mexico come up to have Juan personally make their masks.

Juan has a very interesting collection of Luchadores masks. Many of these are signed by their owners and were given to Juan after their matches. They adorn his shop, a collector's dream. The autographed masks of El Santo, Blue Demon, Rey Mysterio Jr., and others stare down at entering customers. 💀

ABOVE: Don't call him "chicken". . .

4

The Match

Who's Who?

IF THEY WRESTLE *Lucha style, all wrestlers are called Luchadores, but only* masked *wrestlers are called enmascarados. In American wrestling your hero is never called your hero; that is too blasé. He is called the "babyface" or just the "face," probably because heroes are supposed to have that boyish charm of innocence about them. In the same way, the bad guy or villain is never the bad guy or villain; he is the "heel." All American pro-wrestling bookers and matchmakers use this terminology when booking a match.*

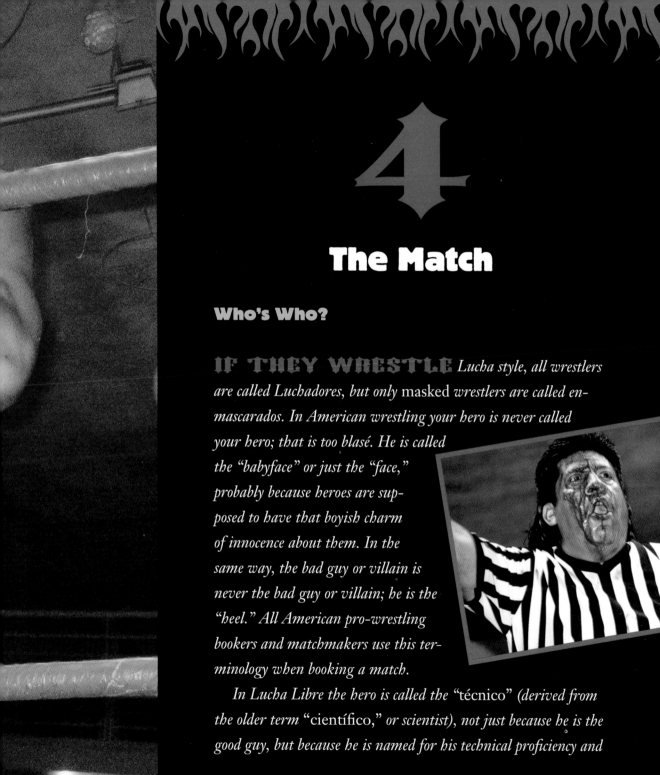

In Lucha Libre the hero is called the "técnico" (derived from the older term "científico," or scientist), not just because he is the good guy, but because he is named for his technical proficiency and

RIGHT: "Comin' at ya!" **ABOVE:** Even the referees aren't safe in Lucha

style and strict adherence to the rules and conduct of Lucha (a kind of Goody Two-Shoes). The bad guy is the *"rudo."* How simple can it get? He is rude. The rudo is a brawler, a rule breaker: nasty, mean and unrepentant. A great rudo or heel will dictate the pace of the match.

As in North American wrestling, técnicos and rudos will sometimes reverse roles—the good guy will take a bad turn, the bad guy has a change of heart, and then the next thing you know, the camps have changed and you have a whole new perspective on the match. In a business sense this is a smart move; after a Luchador has feuded with his arch nemesis for several matches you switch around the emotional motivation, and the fans are looking at a whole new match with the same participants. If you have followed wrestlers throughout the years, you can track their rise to good guy status and their decline into villainy. It also makes for a more complete and complex wrestler or Luchadore—not everyone is a good guy all the time.

Another important factor in the Lucha match is the third man in the ring, the referee. Like Luchadores who are técnicos and rudos, referees can be either técnicos or rudos. This component is unique in Mexican wrestling. The concept of refs taking sides exists in North American wrestling, but for the most part it is the referee's "incompetence" or lack of attention or the fact that he has been knocked out that allows for times when the rules are flagrantly broken. But in Lucha Libre the referee is a main part of the action; and because there is often more than four or more men battling in the ring, there will be two referees, one good and one bad. It is not uncommon for a referee to get caught up in the physicality of the match and take a few "bumps" of his own.

Rules

The rules of Lucha Libre are not that different from American professional wrestling. Victory can be achieved by pinning your opponent's shoulders to the mat for a three count. Another way is to make your opponent submit. This is usually done from a submission hold, and another way is to knock your opponent out of the ring (if he doesn't get back in by the count of twenty he loses). Many times the referee counts at a very leisurely pace to get to twenty. I've been

at a few matches where one Luchador was knocked out of the ring and the ref started counting to twenty. At six I got up, went to the bathroom, got some tacos, a beer, stopped to talk to a friend on the way back to my seat, and when I sat back down the ref was at eleven. And victory can also be achieved by disqualification. Using the ropes for leverage is illegal and grounds for disqualification, as is, if Luchadores fight into the ropes and one man should become tangled up—the other Luchador may not attempt to pin him. Instead the referee breaks up the action and releases the trapped Luchador.

A Luchador can also be disqualified if he attempts an illegal hold or move such as the very dangerous Martinete. We know this in American wrestling as a pile driver or tombstone. Taz, a former ECW champion, had his neck broken in one of these moves and still continued to wrestle until the match was over. If a Luchador hits his opponent in the groin, he will be disqualified; if a Luchador has outside interference, he can be disqualified (this rule gets a little confusing during tag team matches); if a Luchador hits, kicks, or attacks the referee in any way, he gets disqualified. And if a Luchador tries to rip his opponent's mask completely off, he can be disqualified.

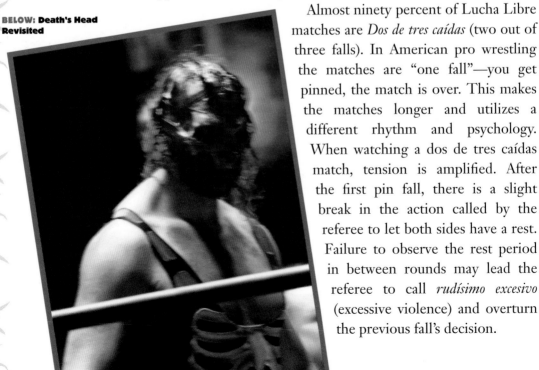

BELOW: **Death's Head Revisited**

Almost ninety percent of Lucha Libre matches are *Dos de tres caídas* (two out of three falls). In American pro wrestling the matches are "one fall"—you get pinned, the match is over. This makes the matches longer and utilizes a different rhythm and psychology. When watching a dos de tres caídas match, tension is amplified. After the first pin fall, there is a slight break in the action called by the referee to let both sides have a rest. Failure to observe the rest period in between rounds may lead the referee to call *rudísimo excesivo* (excessive violence) and overturn the previous fall's decision.

Psychology

The dos de tres caídas is structured for maximum fan participation. Imagine your favorite wrestler (técnico) is battling away against some despicable foe (rudo), and all of a sudden he gets pinned (and usually by some nefarious way of cheating on his opponent's part). Now the crowd is really vested in the physical and psychological story that is unfolding in front of them. If their guy gets pinned again it's over. So with baited breath the fans watch as their guy battles back from a deficit, and before you know it—BAM!!—the hero pins the bad guy. The score is even, the tension builds. The next pin fall determines victory and defeat. This is the classic setup; this is classic storytelling. A smart match has a narrative psychology behind it. To the average viewer, it's two men fighting in the center of the ring, but a skillful Luchadore tells a story every move. With various holds and reverses, he builds toward your climax. He keeps the audience involved, he spins an epic through his actions—ups and downs.

ABOVE: On a one-way trip to the canvas

The hero is in peril, the crowd gets behind him; the hero starts making a comeback, the crowd cheers him on; the rudo halts his comeback, and the crowd's emotions start to go back and forth. Over and over again, the hero fights his way out of peril, but with treacherous moves, the rudo keeps digging a deeper and deeper hole for our técnico to crawl out from. That is what is considered ring psychology, and some wrestlers are masters at this—the timing, pacing and the dictating of the overall emotional feel to a match. Most importantly, the best wrestlers mesmerize the fans. All of these skills come after years of experience. The Luchadores know they must keep the audience involved; they must have the fans vested in *this* match, either cheering for the técnico or jeering for the rudo. Emotional empathy is one of the cornerstones of successful matchmaking.

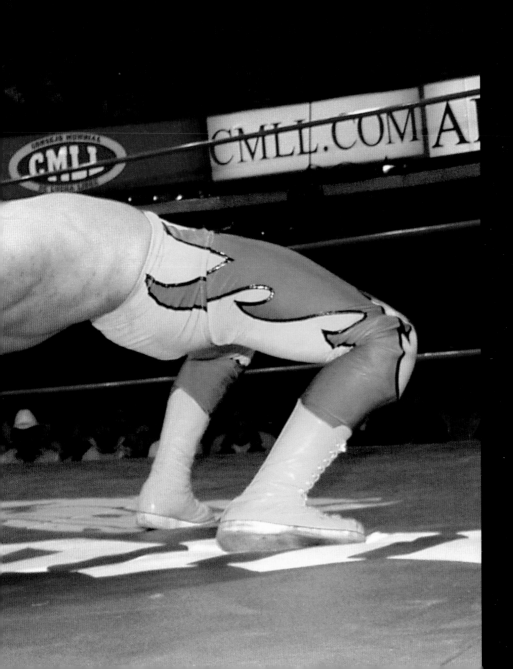

Style

The main style that is used in Lucha Libre is an aerial style that employs more "high spots" than American professional wrestling, or even the Mexican-influenced Japanese wrestling. The "high spots" are just what they sound like, moves that are so acrobatic that they seem to defy gravity as well as logic—some of these guys have to be crazy to attempt these moves. Most of the Mexican Luchadores are not as large as their North American counterparts. Although some of the Luchadores in the past and present have incredibly athletic physiques, not many have achieved the overly muscular build that has taken hold in American wrestling today. Many of the wrestlers in North America spend several years in the gym bodybuilding—they have access to better training facilities, food, and drugs. They have the advantage when it comes to nutrition and supplements, but not desire and skill. It seems fitting that the average Luchador has the physique of an athletically developed but not monstrous-sized man. It fits with the concept of the enmascarado being one of the people.

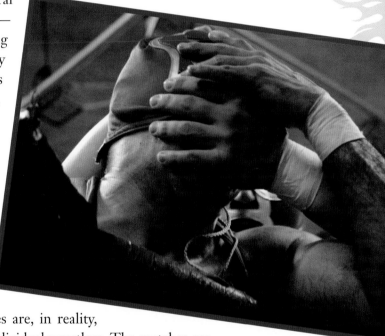

ABOVE: "NO-NO!!"

LEFT: This is why ringside seats cost extra: high flying tax

Just as a majority of the single matches will be dos de tres caídas, most of the matches are, in reality, between teams instead of the individual wrestlers. The matches are either two against two or tag teams called "*parejas*" or three-on-three matches with teams called "*trios*" (sometimes called *tercias*). Those are the most common. These six-man tag matches are also known as "*relevos australianos*" (Australian tag match), and teams of four are called "*atómicas*" (sometimes known as *cuartetos*). These matches of four against four are called "*relevos atómicos.*" With this shuffling around of técnicos versus rudos you can have an almost unlimited supply of good battling evil. Sometimes, to really pique the crowd's interest, técnicos may team up with rudos to fight together; these are called *"parejas increíbles."* The multitag team elimination matches are known as *"torneos cibernéticos."*

The Mask in the Match

The mask (máscara) creates intrigue. Once a wrestler puts on the mask, it takes over his personality. It either has a life of its own, or the mask unleashes a part hidden deep within the Luchador's psyche that he has tried to keep hidden. Wearing the mask allows the Luchador a sense of freedom, to be who he wants to be, and how he wants to act comes alive. The mask signifies and objectifies the persona of the Luchador. Whatever inhibitions or fears are felt by the wrestler, the mask overcomes them. It is fetishistic and fevered, but liberating—not only for the Luchador but for the fans. The mask is the single most important thing in an enmascarado's life.

BELOW: A bloodied Los Villanos

OPPOSITE: Atlantis holds a prized possession: the *máscara* of a fallen adversary

Luchas de apuestas (matches with wagers) were created to bring an added element of intrigue to the matches. Contestants now wouldn't just be fighting for a "W" in the win column—they would be battling to keep their honor. The most extreme of these luchas de apuesta is a *"máscara contra máscara"* (mask vs. mask) match. This is the pinnacle of masked wrestling matches; the winner has the power to unmask the loser! To pit not only one's mask but identity against another enmascarado's is the ultimate risk and offers the possibility of the ultimate prize. Picture Spider-Man fighting Batman, and the loser has to be exposed to the world. Careers have actually been ruined overnight when an enmascarado's true identity was announced publicly. It wasn't just his face that was shown; traditionally the loser has to openly announce who he is and where he is from, exposing

everything about his hidden persona that he had kept secretly for so long. In a bizarre way, the winner of the match absorbs the vanquished enmascarado's mystique, all the mystery, history, all the glory of the loser's past matches and career transmutes into the victor's persona. The taking of another enmascarado's mask is the most humiliating and heartbreaking match to compete in, for both the técnico and rudo. Many fabled enmascarados and Luchadores have trophy cases lined with the colorful masks of their exposed and fallen competitors. It was said that El Santo's trophy case was of museum quality with all the masks he had garnered in his long career in the ring, like a big game hunter lining his den with the stuffed heads of all his conquests. Enmascarado legends collect their opponents' identities as if they were coveted skins of mystical beasts.

There are also *"cabellera contra cabellera"* (hair vs. hair) matches. This is the equivalent of the máscara contra máscara match with participants who don't wear masks—instead they lose their hair, akin to a public scalping. The loser has his head shaved and could be forced to leave town. In reality, the loser would work different venues for a while until his hair grew back, and he returned to the arena where he was shaved to start a new feud with the guy who shaved him bald. Now you ask, what happens if an unmasked Luchador fought an enmascarado? That would be a "cabellera contra máscara" (hair vs. mask) match with the same results for the loser. Beating your enemy isn't good enough; public humiliation and professional shame seem to be par for the course.

I have seen several cabellera contra cabellera matches. There is always a lot of talk on the microphone after the match between the winner and loser and toward the crowd. These arguments get very heated and most of the time the subject matter finds its way into the vein of the winner's mother performing some morally objectionable act of depravity to a barnyard animal (seriously). I do not speak Spanish, but I have stood next to fans who were enjoying the show and asked random people what was being said. I gradually pieced together quite the colorful vocabulary of disparaging phrases. Verbal humiliation is also par for the course.

Movers and Shakers

Okay, you sit down to watch a match and you see all the wild, over-the-top moves and maneuvers being performed before you. If you are a novice you have no clue what is happening in front of you. So let's take a few lines to explain some of the more famous moves in Lucha Libre:

Suicida (suicide): The name given to any number of crazy moves that result in a Luchadore flying out of the ring.

Desnucadora: One of many ways to perform the powerbomb.

Plancha (ironing board): A flying cross bodypress, finishing move that comes off the top ropes or turnbuckle.

Tornillo: Plancha with a full twist around the axis from the top turnbuckle to the outside of the ring, sometimes called the *suicida plancha.*

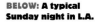

BELOW: A typical Sunday night in L.A.

Tope: A headbutt.

Suplex con Puente: A German suplex that is followed up with a winning pin.

Centón or *Sentón* (blanket): Covering the opponent with the back bump after coming down hard with a splash.

Rana estilo Pino: A Jackknife hold.

Patadas voladoras: Drop kick.

La filomena: A spin kicking.

Tapatía paseada: A rolling Romero Special.

La Calabaza: A Pendulum Submission hold.

La Gongorina: A modified Mexican stretch.

Tijeras: Swinging toss maneuver.

Guillotina: A leg drop from high up, crashing down on the opponent's neck.

Cuatro or *Cruceta:* A figure four leg lock.

Rana: Pinning the opponent's shoulders on the mat for a three count using the Luchador's legs to hold the opponent down.

Huracánrana: A move invented by Huracán Ramírez, it is basically the same move as above but with an added flying headscissor used before the takedown.

Quebradora: A spinning backbreaker performed off the rope.

Quebradora con reguilete: A spinning backbreaker (sometimes known as a *Quebrador con Grio* or a "Tilt-a-Whirl backbreaker").

Quebradora Lagunera: Double underhook backbreaker submission.

This is only a sampling of maneuvers and holds. Practiced and practiced by the Luchadores until they can do them in their sleep, the style of acrobatic, combative movement literally becomes first nature for these men. Their balance, center of gravity, the way they walk, everything about them undergoes a physical transformation until they are perfect examples of fighting machines. Some of the older Luchadores have been around so long that they've seen almost every variation of a move that is thrown at them. The great ones anticipate these moves and already have a counter move ready to go at the exact second their opponent tries to put a "finishing move" on them.

Every wrestler has a signature move or "finisher." Just as the mask sets him apart from other enmascarados or Luchadores, his "finishing move" sets him apart from the other hundreds of wrestlers working in the business. A finisher, finishing move, or signature move is the move, maneuver, submission, or hold that finishes the match. Once this bad boy is thrown on an opponent, it is over. The finishing move is the number-one weapon in your arsenal. It is the granddaddy of all moves that a Luchador knows—once applied or committed to, victory is almost always assured.

Now, one might ask, "Hey, if that move is *so* devastating, why doesn't a wrestler just run in the ring and throw it on his opponent and finish the match in ten seconds?" Well, they could, and in the States matches like that are called "squash matches" or "enhancement matches." These matches are usually reserved for some up-and-coming wrestler that people are really looking into. A squash match is just what it sounds like: one wrestler "squashes" his opponent very quickly. This fast victory makes the up-and-comer look impressive; if he has several squash matches with named mid-card talent his resume of destruction looks good. Then he's positioning himself to get into a program (feud) with a bigger-name talent and start on a series of hard-fought matches.

In Lucha Libre these types of matches are rare, first of all because Lucha Libre has the "two out of three falls" system of wrestling. A Luchador may get pinned quickly once, but he has time to gather his wits about him and start the match again once the ref has called the match to commence. Also, in Lucha Libre, Luchadores don't just want to beat their opponents quickly, they want to bring them to the brink of

LEFT: **One way to work the kinks out of your neck**

physical, emotional, and psychological depilation. No one wants to beat an opponent without delivering some physical punishment along the way—the harder fought the battle, the sweeter the taste of victory.

If a Luchador were to go into match after match and lay waste to all his opponents—and worse, if *everyone* had this mind-set—instead of the three-hour wrestling card you'd get fifteen minutes of violence. Fans don't want to see just that. And promoters definitely don't want to have matches where the fans respond negatively. They have to guarantee fans get what they paid to see, and that they will pay in the future to watch the live events.

So who has a signature move and what is it? Gory Guerrero, one of the founders of Lucha and a master technician, had various moves he used to finish off his opponents. So powerful was his influence that several moves have been named after him, one being the "Gory Bomb." But what types of moves exist, and how many of them are out there?

Just as complex as a thousand different chess matches going on at once, there are thousands upon thousands of moves and variations of the standard moves in Lucha Libre. Whole careers have been spent studying them; like shooting pool, no shot is the same. Let's take a look at some Luchadores and some of the finishing moves they are known for.

Eddie Guerrero would finish his opponents from a "Top Turn-buckle Frog Splash" (this was the finishing move that his late partner Art Barr would use; Eddie used it in honor of his fallen comrade. Eddie also liked to use the "Swinging DDT" when he wrestled as the Black Tiger in Mexico); L. A. Park likes to use a "Highspeed Sunset Flip"; Rey Bucanero likes the "Top Rope Powerbomb"; Perro Aguayo Jr. prefers to render his opponents unconscious using the double foot stomp "La Lanza"; Negro Casas uses a move his father made popular, "La Casita" (known in America as "La Magistral"); the Blue Panther is partial to the "Fujiwara Armbar"; the "Flying Somersault DDT" is used by Villano IV; Hector Garza has been known to finish off his opponents using the "Off the Top Rope Corkscrew Body Press Suicida"; Shocker likes the "Apron Dive Drop Kick" as well as the

"Corkscrew Elbow Drop"; the "Swinging Snap Ring Rope Clothesline" is used by Sangre Azteca; Rey Mysterio Jr. uses the "Somersault Flying Headscissors Suicida" and "West Coast Pop," but the crowd goes crazy for his famous "619" (named in honor of his home area code); El Hijo del Santo ends matches when he throws on "El Caballo" (the "Camel Clutch," which Dr. Wagner Jr. uses on occasion); Averno does a hybrid move that is part "Pedigree" and part "Piledriver," all devastating.

Mephisto is another one that favors the "Powerbomb"; Atlantis has had good success using the spinning torture rack known as "La Atlantida";

Satánico takes sadistic pleasure in applying "El Nudo" (which is a variation on the standing "Figure Four Leg Lock"); Vampiro likes the "Michinoko Driver" (which is a crossface submission); Black Warrior uses the "Nudo Lagunero" and the "Tope Suicida"; Super Astro likes the "Springboard Headbutt"; Kato Kung Lee was known for his "Arm Drag with Leg Throw"; El Samurai and Super Crazy have both used the "Swinging Inverted Facelock DDT" with the same victorious results; the "Springboard Somersault Drop Kick" has been used by Juventud Guerrera for years; the famed El Santo liked the "Back Mounted Chinlock" (El Hijo del Santo liked this as well); Dr. Wagner Jr. has taken many out with his "Hammerlock

with Neck Submission" move; Felino uses the "Angled Reverse Figure Four Leg Lock"; Sugi Sito preferred a "Medio Cangrejo" (which is a half Boston crab); Mil Máscaras liked the "Standing Surfboard"; then there's the "Step over Armbar Cradle (which is another name for La Magistral), which the Luchador Heavy Metal decided to rename the "Heavy Metal Cradle"; not to be outdone, El Dandy would do his own stylized version of La Magistral and call it "Dandina"; the "Forward Leg Sweep Cradle" was used by Espectro; the "Cruceta Invertida" (Reverse Figure Four Leg Lock) was used by Tigre Blanco; Máscara Sagrada would use

OPPOSITE: The Human
Tornado heads into
the audience at a
Lucha VaVoom Show

an abdominal stretch known as "Enredadera"; Charro Aguayo used to like putting people to sleep using "La Mecedora" (the Rocking Chair); Fishman used a kangaroo dropkick called "Patadas de Canguro"; Hector Guerrero put the "Jalapeño Roll" to good use. Even Gory's grandson, Chavo Guerrero Jr., uses the "Gory Lock Face First Slam."

How good does a ring announcer have to be to call a match in a wrestling lexicon filled with hundreds of names of hundreds of moves? He has to be just as versed in the action and moves as the wrestlers are to call the match the way it is unfolding in the ring. Just as there is one signature move for one wrestler, seeing that a majority of the matches are either two against two or three against three, many times wrestlers will do a double variation on one move when they are both in the ring at the same time: The "Double Press Slam Gutbuster Drop" is a favorite of Los Villanos; "The Double Super Crucifix Powerbomb" is the preferred method of mayhem of Las Cachorras Orientales; and the "Double Press Slam Ring Rope Clothesline Drop" has been perfected by the tag team of Dantes and Universo 2000. And of course, once again, there are dozens upon dozens of these double team finishing moves, but that doesn't end there.

Some tag teams don't want to do the same moves in unison; each member wants to use his particularly devastating finishing move to its full advantage, so they execute "finishing combination moves" that combine two or more different finishing moves in a sequence. So one team can do an "Inverted Back Breaker Rack" that is finished with the "Off the Top Rope Elbow Smash." Los Gringos Locos would go from a "Shoulder Mount Suplex" right into an "Off the Top Rope Huracánrana" without missing a beat; the team of Dr. Wagner Jr. and Shocker go from the "Camel Clutch," which lays an opponent out, to "Springboard Dropkick." The teams have to have an almost telepathic relationship between each other to anticipate each other's moves. But with years of training, traveling and wrestling with one's partner, you develop the symbiotic relationship that is needed for victory. A good partner can sense and see when his partner is going in for the kill, and he is ready to pounce.

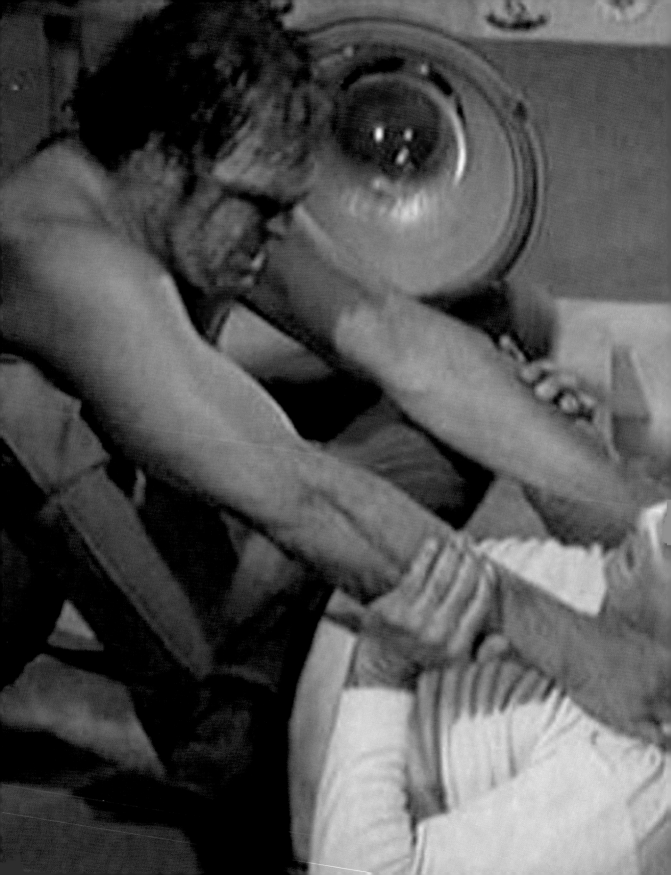

5

> "Then the lid was raised and we saw those precious relics of the Masked Prophet."
>
> —Sax Rohmer, *The Mask of Fu Manchu*

Los Enmascarados
(The Masked Men)

AS I NOTED earlier in my dissertation of devastation, my magnum opus of masked mayhem, there are three top dogs in the history of Lucha Libre, a trio of enmascarados who have blazed the way for all Lucha fans throughout the world. Let's start with the boss daddy of the bunch, El Santo.

El Santo

There were other enmascarados before El Santo and others since he has gone, but no one will match his impact on Lucha Libre. El Santo was the man; his importance to the

OPPOSITE: Santo battling just another one of hundreds of ghoulish henchmen he faced in more than fifty films   ABOVE: "Don't even think about it, lady. No one takes Santo's *máscara* off, not even for a little afternoon delight . . ."

sport cannot be understated. El Santo's shadow still falls warmly over his legions of fans from beyond the grave. What Muhammad Ali was to boxing, what Schwarzenegger was to bodybuilding, what Hulk Hogan was to North American professional wrestling, and what Michael Jordan was to basketball, so El Santo was to Lucha Libre. El Santo fought for years behind a silver mask, and he was called El Enmascarado de Plata.

El Santo was a real-life superhero that the fans could see, touch, hear, and speak to. He was one of their own. Unlike his American superhero counterparts Superman, Spider-Man, Batman or any other adjective-laden-named man, Santo never revealed his true identity behind the mask. The fans did not know his face or name or origins. Everyone north of the border knows the identity of Clark Kent, Peter Parker, and Bruce Wayne, but El Santo carefully and meticulously kept his identity secret for a reason. The fans not only loved El Santo the man, El Santo the wrestler, but they came to love El Santo the symbol.

Santo symbolized all the qualities of heroism: righteousness, bravery, strength, compassion, and loyalty. Every aspect that went into making a hero or legend became an integral part of Santo's style. Santo not only displayed these brave traits in the ring but he showed them time after time in movies and comic books and on television.

El Santo descended from the wrestling heavens on September 23, 1917, and was christened into the world of the mere mortal as Rodolfo Guzmán Huerta in Tulancingo, Hidalgo, Mexico. It wasn't until the mid-1930s that a still very young Huerta entered into the ranks of Lucha Libre. First wrestling under his own name, Rudy Guzmán (as a rudo no less!), Huerta got his first taste of the world he would one day come to command. Some of the older Santo fans I got to know refuse to acknowledge their hero was, at one time, a bad guy.

Huerta quickly changed to the style of the masked wrestler and took the moniker "El Murciélago II" (The Bat II). Not finding much success as El Murciélago II, and with the original owner of the name El Murciélago not being too keen on having a doppelganger floating around the business (which would confuse fans and take money out of El Murciélago's pockets), Huerta opted to become "El Hombre

Rojo," (The Red Man). He had some success with the name El Hombre Rojo, but not the type of success and admiration he hoped and trained hard for. The story of Santo being called up to the big time is often accredited to EMLL's talent scout Jesús "Chucho" Lomelí, who had the foresight to see the untapped greatness in Huerta. But many people believe it was Texas-born tough guy Jack O'Brien, who first saw Huerta wrestling in Pachuca as Rudy Guzmán and was so impressed with both him and his brother Miguel "Black" Guzmán that he told Lomelí not to let these two prospects get away.

Even though Huerta was in the big leagues with EMLL, that didn't mean he didn't have to work hard anymore; if anything he had to wrestle and train harder to prove to everyone that he not only belonged there but he was going to stay.

All that hard work and sacrifice paid off in 1942. Competing in a brutal eight-man Battle Royale in Mexico City, the Mecca of masked wrestling, he came out victorious. Not only did he win the match, he was reborn as El Santo. From that night on, El Santo's career and the world of Lucha Libre would never be the same.

Santo usually weighed in at a very fit and muscular 215 to 220 pounds and was said to be around six feet tall. Judging by some photos and old matches, it seems that the promoter may have added an inch or two to Santo's height.

During his illustrious career Santo won a slew of wrestling titles. When Santo partnered with the famed Gory Guerrero, a wrestler he had feuded with in some classic struggles, the pair created the legendary team that would become known as "La Pareja Atómica"

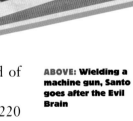

ABOVE: Wielding a machine gun, Santo goes after the Evil Brain

CINEMATOGRAFICA CALDERON, S. A.
Y SANTO EL ENMASCARADO DE PLATA
presentan a:

SANTO
EL ENMASCARADO DE PLATA

ARMANDO SILVESTRE
JULIO ALDAMA
MARY MONTIEL
GREGORIO CASSALS

presentación de: IVONNE GOVEA

ANTO CONTRA S JINETES L TERROR

A COLORI

nento: JESUSS VELAZQUEZ QUINTERO
raina: RENE CCARDONA y JESUS VELAZQUEZ QUINTERO

Dirección: RENE CARDONA J

(The Atomic Pair). They were just that, blinding with their speed and devastating with their power. With their combined strengths and techniques, they forged themselves into a highly explosive fighting unit that dominated throughout the decade.

And it was during this time, when he and Gory reigned over the Lucha world, that some of his most famous matches took place, when La Pareja Atómica squared off against heated rivals "Los Hermanos Shadow" (the team of Black Shadow and Blue Demon). The bloody brutality of that match is still talked about today by Lucha purists as one of the all-time best. On November 7, 1952, at the Arena Coliseo, Santo faced Black Shadow in the now-classic máscara contra máscara match; after three falls Black Shadow lost his mask to Santo.

Santo became more than a wrestling superstar, he transcended into a cultural icon with movies the fans loved to go see and comic books that sold millions and were read by everyone. He was the most popular in the ring, on the screen, and in the comics; he was the first king of all media.

Most of his films are not great gems in cinematic history, but what they lack in structure and style, they make up for in creativity and outrageousness. With titles like *Cerebro del Mal* (Brain of Evil) and *La Furia de los Karatekas* (The Fury of the Karate Experts), it is unlikely that any of these movies are going to knock *Citizen Kane* off its lofty perch on the tree of movie greats. But can Citizen Kane battle zombies, vampires, Aztec mummies and Martians late at night after battling in the ring all day? I doubt it. Don't pick up a Santo film and look for deep meaningful relationships between males and females, man's inner journey to find his true self, or the quiet reflective ponderings of youthful angst. But if you want to see a guy in a silver mask kick the daylights out of a werewolf or the living dead using flying leg drops and headbutts, well, Santo is the man for the job.

El Santo married twice. His wives were named Maria de los Ángeles Rodríguez and Eva Enriqueta Vallejo Vadager (Mara). He had ten children with his first wife, and with his second wife he had one more, bringing the El Santo fold to a whopping eleven kids. The mystique of Santo followed him throughout his career. Everyone wanted to know who Santo was and yet no one wanted

RODOLFO
GUZMAN
HUERTA
EL SANTO

191   1984

Santo unmasked, if that makes sense. The illusion that Santo was an unknown avenger who could easily hide among the masses when his mask was off was still very appealing to the public. It is like watching a magic trick: We know it is a trick but we don't want to know how it is done; we just want to sit back and enjoy the performance. But public speculation came to an end when an unprecedented and totally spur of the moment event took place. During the filming of Mexican TV show *Contrapunto* on January 26, 1984, Santo publicly unmasked himself on national television.

Although many fans had already known Santo's real name and history, this action seemed to be Santo's way of saying farewell to all the fans who loved him and watched him perform for decades to sold-out arenas and packed movie theaters, and a prophetic good-bye it was. . . . Santo died from a heart attack one week later on February 5, 1984, at 9:40 P.M. The Luchador of Luchadores was sixty-six years old. It has been said it was the biggest funeral in Mexico's history. Like the enmascarado he was in life, he was buried wearing his famous silver mask.

El Demonio Azúl

(BLUE DEMON)

Batman. The Lone Ranger. Spider-Man. Superheroes who hide their identity from the world while they battle the forces of evil and injustice. These heroic strongmen were willing to put their own safety at risk to help others. In Lucha Libre, these heroes do live, they do exist, larger than life—in flesh and blood and brawn and brains. In the world of Lucha Libre, giants like these walk among mortals. In the Golden Era of Lucha Libre in Mexico three such demigods ruled the ring. The blazing triumvirate of El Santo, Blue Demon, and Mil Máscaras has forever seared the ideal of the enmascarado into the public's mind.

OPPOSITE: *Blue Demon* comic book cover

BELOW: **Blue Demon delivers a brutal over-the-knee backbreaker**

This holy trinity of Mexican wrestling starred in over a combined two hundred movies, competed in thousands of matches and graced the covers of countless magazines and comic books. Wrestling superstars of today would not be where they are now if it wasn't for the careers of these men and those like them. WWE superstar Eddie Guerrero and Rey Mysterio not only were inspired by El Santo, Blue Demon, and Mil Máscaras but followed in their footsteps. Both Guerrero and Mysterio come from a long and respected lineage of Luchadores famed throughout Mexico.

The one in this heroic trio who seems to get lost in the shuffle of fame and notoriety is the Blue Demon. A fan favorite and Mexican wrestling movie star in his own right, Demon's legend (like his two contemporaries El Santo and Máscaras) is sacrosanct in his native country.

The Blue Demon was spawned on April 24, 1922. He was christened Alejandro Muñoz Moreno. The fifth of twelve children, he lived in Villa de García, a small town in Nuevo Leon. He spent his

MEDICO
ASESINO

SOMBRA
VENGADORA

STICIEROS

PRESENTA
TINIEB
EL GIGAN

INVITADOS ESPE
ELSA CARDEN
DAVID SILV

BLACK
SHADOW

N FEDERICO CURIEL - FOTOGRAFIA JOSE O. RAMOS - ARGUMENTO

early years around Los Rodríguez, Coahuila. School was not Demon's forte; he loved music and wanted to pursue a career as a musician. He decided to drop out of high school and follow his musical muse against the protest of his father, who was an agriculturist, and who wanted his son to continue his schooling. But Demon felt the allure of a mariachi lifestyle was too strong to compete with academics. Unfortunately, having a love of music does not guarantee the talent to go with it. Demon's early efforts in music were met with failure. After the disappointment of not making it as a musician, Demon started to experience a certain amount of wanderlust. He ended up in Monterrey with some relatives. This is where the music world lost a would-be player and the universe of Lucha Libre gained a superstar.

It was in Monterrey where Demon befriended Franklin Hernández while they were working in a railway station. Hernández was the brother to Luchador star Rolando Vera. Vera must have been very excited when he came upon the young Moreno, a handsome, strapping youth who had natural athletic ability. Vera decided to train the young Demon, refraining from teaching him the world of the Luchador just yet. He conditioned the youngster—building his strength, endurance, coordination, and balance. When Vera finally brought Demon into the world of amateur wrestling, Demon did more than handle himself competently by compiling an undefeated record. But Vera still kept the secretive world of the Luchador at arm's length from the youth. Being in top physical shape and training in combative sports is one thing, but the world of professional wrestling has always been a guarded secret by the participants. Before a seasoned professional starts to teach a prospect the ins and outs of this world, he wants to make sure that this is not just a passing fancy for some starry-eyed youngster.

The love, dedication and discipline that goes into professional wrestling is unlike that of any other sport; the wrestlers and Luchadores live and breathe it. This is not a job; it is a calling, a way of life. Luchadores do not live the nine-to-five lifestyle, they are Luchadores 24/7, always. It doesn't matter if they are in the ring or on the street, the Luchador walks and talks the life with pride and dignity;

it is an exclusive membership, and entrance into it is guarded and held in the highest esteem.

After training for some time Vera knew this willing youngster had something special in the making. He revealed to Demon the ropes of the Lucha Libre world, but Demon's debut was not under the demonic nom de guerre; he wrestled under his real name. On March 31, 1948, his first opponent and first victory was against Chema López. This was the start of a long and illustrious career for the Demon.

It was Vera who came up with the idea of the young Moreno wearing an azure-colored mask and cape and using the name "Blue Demon." Demon liked the way it sounded, but more importantly he trusted Vera's experience and guidance, and in his first match as the newly renamed Blue Demon he scored a win over Benny Aricilla.

He worked days in the Monterrey railway stations as Alejandro Muñoz Moreno and wrestled nights as the Blue Demon. Wrestling talent scout Jesús Lomelí, who by chance happened to catch one of Demon's performances one night, changed everything. Lomelí was so impressed in what he saw in the young man—the same skills and intensity that Vera saw—he offered Demon the chance to come wrestle in the Mecca of all Lucha Libre wrestling, Mexico City.

Vera wanted his protégé's Mexico City debut to be extraordinary so he intensified Demon's training regime. Hour after hour was spent sweating and battling in hot, stuffy gyms. Vera also wanted to stress something else to the young man, how to behave in Mexico City. This was not like any other city Demon had performed in and

Vera wanted to be sure that his student knew what to expect in the ring and how to handle himself in the tough streets of Mexico City. In September 1948 the people of Mexico City got their first look at what would become a legendary career with the first appearance of Blue Demon. He lost his first match.

Demon lost his Mexico City debut to Ciclón Veloz because of disqualification. The loss didn't matter, though. What was important was that Demon made an impact on the fans. Demon's demeanor in the start of his career was that of a rudo. This villainous persona suited Demon well in the beginning, and he was able to leave his daytime job in the railway stations in Monterrey and move to Mexico City to become a full-time Luchador.

OPPOSITE: Blue
Demon hooks up with
stunning Mexican
beauty Maura Monti
in this 1968 cinematic
venture

Blue Demon fought for several years as a wrestler the fans loved to hate. Night after night Demon had to go out and provoke the crowds to despise every move he made in the ring, so they loved the técnico even more. And Demon, along with other enmascarados, had to do this with his face hidden behind a mask. An actor's most visible asset is his face, and his or her ability to convey pain, fear, joy, rage, horror and love is first expressed in a facial reaction. To have the ability to project the same emotions from behind a mask, and through body movements and well-executed wrestling moves, is an art form unto itself.

In 1953 Blue Demon turned técnico and started a long-running feud with one of the country's leading rudos at the time: El Santo! Blue Demon teamed with another colorfully named wrestler, Black Shadow (Alejandro Cruz Ortiz), and became "Los Hermanos Shadow." They were billed as "brothers," a common practice of inventing family connections between wrestling tag team partners so that the inevitable breakup of the team leads to some heated sibling rivalries and big money matches. El Santo was teamed up with Gory Guerrero (the legendary father of Latino Heat, Eddie Guerrero), and the two teams had some of the most ferocious matches in Mexico— always in front of full-capacity houses.

Demon and El Santo didn't step into the ring as single competitors until August 1953, but when they did they brought the house down. Demon defeated El Santo in their first solo encounter and that gave Demon Number Contender Status and a chance at El Santo's NWA Championship. In their second match, this time for the title, Blue Demon once again defeated the masked man in silver and won his first championship at the Arena Coliseo. Demon defeated his title bravely until he lost it to Karloff Lagarde almost five years later.

Being in Lucha Libre is a dangerous occupation. The human body is not meant to take that much punishment on a daily basis, and no matter how athletic a Luchador is, no matter how well the match is planned out, accidents happen. Luchadores have to have faith that the opponent they are going against is well-trained and experienced with the art of in-ring conflict. The object is to defeat the opponent, not kill them or leave them permanently damaged (although if you

RIGHT: A great piece of trivia: the director of this movie, Chano Urueta, had a acting role in Sam Peckinpah's *The Wild Bunch*

Filmica Vergara
(CINECOMISIONES. S.A) presenta

COLUMBIA PICTURES

PROD. DE
LUIS ENRIQUE
VERGARA C.
ARGUMENTO:
RAFAEL GARCIA
TRAVESI S
FERNANDO
OSES

JE DEMON
DEMONIO AZUL

con

BLUE DEMON
Jaime **FERNANDEZ**
Rosa Maria **VAZQUEZ**
Mario **OREA**

ALTIA MICHEL · FERNANDO OSES · CESAR GAY
LOBO NEGRO · IVONNE GOBEA · VICTOR
JORDAN

looked at some of the famous storylines you'd think that mayhem was the only object). But pain is a constant reminder of how rough the wrestling world is.

Virtually every wrestler has been injured at one time or another during his career, and Blue Demon was no exception to this painful rule. In 1957, while battling El Espectro, Demon fractured his skull after colliding headfirst into the metal ring post. The injury took a toll on Demon but several months later, after rehab and reconditioning, he was back in action. On his return Demon left the EMLL (the Mexican equivalent to the WWE) and became a free agent. This entitled Demon the chance to wrestle around the world and Demon took full advantage of it. He found new fans all over Mexico and New York City. He even did a tour through the southern United States and traveled all over Latin America. Blue Demon's shadow had now spread far and wide.

But injury once again came to plague Demon. In 1965 in a match against Cavernario Galindo in Oaxaca, Demon's head crashed into the floor of the arena after he was thrown from the ring. After the match Demon collapsed and was rushed to the hospital. He ruptured several blood vessels in his brain. He had refractured his skull, and this time he was out for a year. If you're ever questioned whether wrestling is "real" or not, take a look at some of the medical charts of any wrestler. The scars and bruises that line their bodies are road maps to the hard routes they've traveled from arena to arena. Demon needed time for his body to heal, physically and mentally. An injury as severe as a fractured skull can linger on the psyche longer than the body.

But Demon's hiatus was not wasted—he had temporarily left one arena to conquer another: the fantastic world of Mexican cinema. Like El Santo, who had already starred in several well-known Lucha Libre films, Demon found himself in front of the camera. In 1961, his first time on film was for a movie entitled *La Furia del Ring* (The Fury of the Ring). Although Demon wasn't the star, and his appearance was something of a glorified cameo, the audiences clambered. More films followed, with bigger parts for the Demon. In 1964 Blue Demon starred in the aptly named movie *Demonio Azul.* Then came titles like *Demonio Azul contra el Poder Satánico* or, as it is known in one of its English titles, *Blue Demon vs. The Satanic Power* (Demon's ring rival El Santo has a cameo in the film). *La Sombra del Murciélago* (Shadow of the Bat), *Blue Demon contra Las Arañas Infernales* (Blue Demon vs. The Infernal Spiders) and *Blue Demon contra Las Diabólicas* (Blue Demon vs. The Diabolical Women). This time Demon didn't just battle a rudo—he fought the supernatural, terrors from beyond the grave. Aliens, vampires, mummies, and ghouls, a whole plethora of monstrous adversaries. Demon always found himself coming out on top.

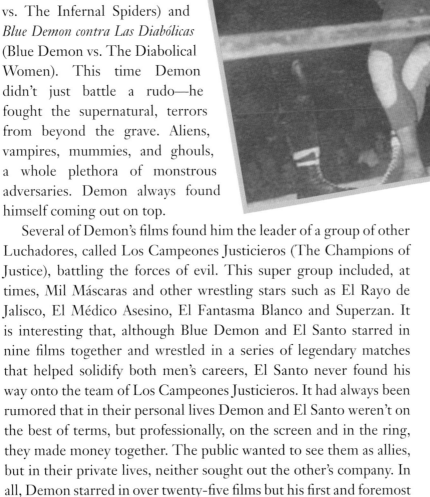

ABOVE: **Blue Demon in battle**

Several of Demon's films found him the leader of a group of other Luchadores, called Los Campeones Justicieros (The Champions of Justice), battling the forces of evil. This super group included, at times, Mil Máscaras and other wrestling stars such as El Rayo de Jalisco, El Médico Asesino, El Fantasma Blanco and Superzan. It is interesting that, although Blue Demon and El Santo starred in nine films together and wrestled in a series of legendary matches that helped solidify both men's careers, El Santo never found his way onto the team of Los Campeones Justicieros. It had always been rumored that in their personal lives Demon and El Santo weren't on the best of terms, but professionally, on the screen and in the ring, they made money together. The public wanted to see them as allies, but in their private lives, neither sought out the other's company. In all, Demon starred in over twenty-five films but his first and foremost love was the ring. His film career was scheduled around his matches

and he continued to be a crowd favorite until he retired in 1988. Even though Demon was out of the spotlight, he kept a hand in the business he loved so dearly, a business he spent over forty years of his life in. He trained other wrestlers, including his son, Blue Demon Jr., and taught them the world of Lucha Libre that he knew so well.

Sadly, Demon passed soon after his retirement from the ring. It wasn't a villainous female vampire that got her fangs on him, or some cursed Aztec mummy that finished our hero, or even a Luchador rival. Natural causes took the Blue Demon from us. The man who honed his body and mind into a finely tuned specimen of Lucha Libre excellence passed away after an early-morning workout. A more fitting way of leaving this mortal coil could not be imagined. Known to his friends and family as Alejandro Muñoz Moreno and known to the world as Blue Demon, he left this world and entered the next on December 16, 2000. He was buried in his beloved blue mask.

Blue Demon Jr.

Like father, like son. And with a father as famous and beloved as the Blue Demon it would be hard for any son not to feel the strain of living in such a colorful shadow, but Demon's offspring decided that the life his father chose was the path that he, too, would take. Like El Hijo del Santo and Los Villanos or the countless others that followed the career paths that their fathers blazed before them, Blue Demon Jr. made his way from behind his father's all-too-familiar image to become his own man but with an identical persona. Like all famous sons of famous fathers, he has become the extension of his dad's mystique and he carries on the *luchística* tradition.

Known as El Hijo de la Leyenda Azul (The Son of the Blue Legend), he started his career in the seventies and soon he lived up to the legend. Engaging in the most brutal of matches, Máscara contra Máscara, he faced and unmasked some pretty tough customers. Enmascarados who lost their in-ring personas to him were Invasor Galáctico, Vendaval, La Mancha, North Panther, Black Panther, Black Killer, La Mosca, Scarlet, Depredador, Síndrome, Gran Sheik, El Jorobado, and Black Demon. Wrestling even today, Demon Jr. entertains and thrills fans all over the world with his familiar azure mask and technical proficiency.

BELOW: **Blue Demon Jr. carrying on his dad's colorful tradition**

Mil Máscaras

"The Man of a Thousand Masks" was born Aaron Rodríguez on July 15, 1942, in San Luis Potosí (although there have been some who say he was actually born in 1939). This third member of the holy trinity of enmascarado greats is a man who still wrestles regularly around the world. Mil is the closest thing to a Lucha icon I have ever seen up close and personal, so it is natural that he is my favorite in many ways. Although it was Santo I first saw in the movies, it was Mil Máscaras that I would watch every Saturday morning. He was there through those formative years when wrestling was the be-all and end-all of things in my life. I've seen him wrestle on television and I've seen him perform live. There was a twenty-five-year space between both outings and the man hadn't missed a beat. . . .

Aaron was an extremely gifted athlete and he excelled in many sports as a youngster: amateur wrestling, judo, baseball and body-building; but his true love was to be in the ring. Not the wrestling ring, but the arena; he wanted to become a bullfighter. His devout mother wasn't keen on the idea of seeing her son gouged by a thousand-pound enraged animal, so she sent him off to a religious seminary school to hopefully put an end to his dreams of becoming a famous toreador. Fate intervened when the bullfighting hopeful went to a Lucha match in 1955 to watch Felipe Ham Lee and Jamaican "Dory" Dixon battle it out. Aaron was so impressed with the muscular Dixon's high-flying abilities in the ring that his aspiration for fighting bulls vanished and was quickly replaced with dreams of fighting a different type of charging animal—Luchadores. The young Aaron continued to train and excel in sports, and in 1963 he was the Freestyle wrestling Champion of Mexico and a top competitor in Judo. He was picked for the national team to represent Mexico in the 1964 Olympics in Tokyo, but a financial problem prevented him from attending, and Aaron had to forgo his dream of winning Olympic gold.

His goal for ring immortality, however, was just around the corner. Having the extensive background in combative sports (the key foundation of any Luchador) and possessing a muscular build, Aaron's next natural step would be into the world of Lucha Libre. Aaron was well versed in kendo, aikido, and karate, and he learned

BELOW: **The Man of a Thousand Masks (and several hundred capes) gets ready for action**

OPPOSITE: **You know that the guy kicking Mil Máscaras in the groin is going to pay for that little indiscretion later on**

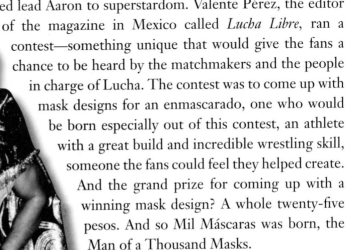

jujitsu from Konde Koma (Mitsuyo Maeda), the man who introduced the now-popular sport to Brazil. He made his debut in 1964 as an unmasked Luchador named Ricardo Durán and wrestled in the smaller venues around Mexico. He had some success, but there was an element missing from Aaron's ring persona. Although he had an impressive physique and expert skills, he knew he needed to incorporate something that would show the entire world what type of Lucha star he had the potential to become.

Fate entered the picture again—not once but twice—and both times helped lead Aaron to superstardom. Valente Pérez, the editor of the magazine in Mexico called *Lucha Libre*, ran a contest—something unique that would give the fans a chance to be heard by the matchmakers and the people in charge of Lucha. The contest was to come up with mask designs for an enmascarado, one who would be born especially out of this contest, an athlete with a great build and incredible wrestling skill, someone the fans could feel they helped create. And the grand prize for coming up with a winning mask design? A whole twenty-five pesos. And so Mil Máscaras was born, the Man of a Thousand Masks.

Aaron Rodríguez would not be the first one to fill those shoes, or, more appropriately, wear that mask. The first man to actually portray the character of Mil Máscaras was a Luchador named Jorge Galindo but he fell out of favor almost immediately. Pérez was lucky enough to have spotted the muscular Ricardo Durán, just who was needed to fill the role of the Man of a Thousand Masks. Mil made his wrestling debut in April 1965 in Guadalajara. To give the newcomer a nice rub, he was teamed with Lucha legend

Black Shadow. From there, he teamed up with El Santo at times, and other Lucha legends as his popularity grew. Aaron Rodríguez was no more. Mil Máscaras was the true personification of the man behind the masks. Mil's style was something that the fans couldn't get enough of either; he out-wrestled his opponents with the skills he had learned in wrestling and judo, or he used some spectacular high-flying move like the *plancha suicida* or the Mexican Surfboard (also called La Tapatía or Romero Special, named after the inventor Rito Romero), or he would just use his incredible strength to render a wrestler helpless with one of his famous bear hugs.

His arsenal of moves and maneuvers far outpaced his opponents', and the fact that he was being taught by the greatest Lucha Libre trainer of all time, Diablo Velazco, didn't hurt either (actually it did hurt—Mil's opponents, that is). Every time he faced an adversary he learned their strengths, their weaknesses, their secrets, their soft spots; he was the complete Luchador, physically challenging and mentally unshakable.

At the same time elsewhere in Mexico, Enrique Vergara, the prolific movie producer, had a problem on his hands. His two top moneymaking masked superstars, Santo and Blue Demon, could not continue to make films for him. His star attraction, El Santo, left his stable over a contract dispute and went to work for other producers. Vergara's second ace in the hole, Blue Demon, was injured severely the year before and his recovery was progressing slowly. His chances of doing a physically demanding action Lucha film were slim. With these two heavy hitters in the genre out of commission, Vergara looked to make a new Lucha superstar that could fulfill contractual obligations and keep his movie-making schedule. But who would be the one to try to follow in the steps of Santo and Demon, two huge stars in both wrestling and cinema? It would have to be someone special, someone unique.

Mil Máscaras was the masked man that Vergara pinned his hopes on. He already knew that Mil was making waves in the world of Lucha, but he hadn't quite broken big-time all across the country . . . yet. Vergara had an idea that would help launch his newest enmascarado hero into stardom and help Mil's Lucha career grow as well. It was simple—the more fans who go to see Mil in the arenas, the more fans who will go to see Mil in the movie theater, a very wise business plan.

Mil Máscaras's first movie role was created specifically to enhance his cinematic mystique, which would echo the Lucha back story that was still being developed, and the personality that Mil would eventually become. It would be an extension of that first starring movie role. But this was a gamble; no one had done it before. Santo and Blue Demon were already established enmascarados superstars and fan favorites before they went into the movies. Their large fan

OPPOSITE: Probably one of the coolest gimmicks around, Mil's leopard *máscara* and matching costume are just plain bad-ass

ABOVE: As it has been done thousands of times over his career, Mil's arms are raised in victory

bases had been firmly established, and producers knew that they were guaranteed a certain box office. But Mil was not yet the breakthrough star he would shortly become and in this, his first real starring movie role, a lot hinged on the outcome.

The movie was called *Mil Máscaras* starring . . . Mil Máscaras! Though this was Mil's first starring role, it wasn't his first time in front of the camera. He had a small part in the film *Los Canallas* early on. Mil's movie career seemed to be one of good luck provided for him by the misfortune of others—notably Santo and Blue Demon, but those two superstars would not be down for long.

The creation myth of Mil in his first movies resembles that of

Spider-Man or Captain America. The hero is created out of tragic happenstance and scientific meddling. The story unfolds in a European war-ravaged wasteland—the body of a dead woman is found, and in her arms she is still clutching her baby, who is miraculously alive. That would be an infant Mil (without the mask). He is taken in by a group of scientists who act as surrogate fathers, and they monitor the young boy's growth while using him as a secret test subject in an experiment to create a superhuman agent to someday pit against aggressive foreign powers. He grows into an incredibly gifted athlete with a superior and vast intellect molded to battle the forces of evil, similar to the American pulp character Doc Savage.

Mil's first film was shot in black and white but his subsequent films were all made in color, the better to display his one thousand masks. He made twenty movies in twenty-five years, and after a long hiatus Mil was back again on the silver screen with the movie *Mil Máscaras vs. the Aztec Mummy*, filmed in 2005.

While all that moviemaking would have been a full-time career for any actor, Mil was still wrestling all around Mexico, and soon he would be traveling all over the world. His official American debut was in Los Angeles in May 1968. He wrestled in the fabled Olympic Auditorium for famed promoter Aileen Eaton (the only woman inducted into the International Boxing Hall of Fame). Ms. Eaton's son, the legendary "Judo" Gene LeBell, grappling master and stuntman extraordinaire, said, "I couldn't believe the amount of people that Máscaras would bring out to the venue, even when the place was regularly being sold out, the lines around the block of fans to even try to get a glimpse of Máscaras coming and going into the arena was staggering."

Mil became so popular that he was the first masked wrestler to headline the famous Madison Square Garden in New York City. He made his Japanese debut on February 19, 1971, defeating Kantaro Hoshino in Tokyo. Mil's name in Japan was "Kamen Kizoku," (The Masked Noble) and the Japanese fans treated him like royalty. In fact, the Japanese wrestlers were so enamored by the mysterious masked Mil that many started to imitate his enmascarado look. The Japanese style of professional wrestling, called *puroresu*, with the added spicy Latin flavor added by Mil, helped metamorphose the sport into a hybrid style called "Luchares," which is still popular today.

The original "Tiger Mask" (Tigre Enmascarado; Satoru Sayama) said of Mil Máscaras's impact in Japan, "Without Mil Máscaras, there would be no other stars that are praised and revered for their excellence in both high-flying and technical wrestling, be it Tiger Mask, The Great Sasuke, Jushin Liger, or Último Dragón. Such was the greatness of his impact in the Orient." Very high praise indeed, as the aforementioned Japanese wrestlers are considered some of the greatest ever to come out of the Land of the Rising Sun.

Mil has battled the best in the world, not only in Mexico but all over the United States and Japan. He has faced legends like "Superstar" Billy Graham, "Classy" Freddie Blassie, Ox Baker, Killer Kowalski, Ken Patera, the Funk Brothers Dory and Terry, Nick Bockwinkle,

OPPOSITE: The international superstar Mil Máscaras is known in Japan as Kamen Kizoku (The Masked Noble)

Jack Brisco, Handsome Harley Race, Billy Robinson, Ivan Koloff, and the list goes on and on.

Mil Máscaras is a true road warrior, traveling all over the world continuously for over thirty years, piling up the air miles and victories and cementing his reputation in the hall of the Lucha Libre legends. Mil has worked for one time or another in all of the biggest wrestling promotions in the world: Michinoku Pro, AJPW, WAR, CMLL, AAA, WCW, and WWE (WWWF). Anywhere there were wrestling fans in the world, Mil traveled to entertain them. He won numerous international championships. There must be something in the Máscaras bloodline because Mil has two real-life brothers (not the gimmick sibling relationship set up between Blue Demon and the Black Shadow) who have had long and successful careers themselves. Dos Caras and El Sicodélico have both followed proudly in their famous brother's footsteps.

Mil Máscaras has transcended the international world of professional wrestling like no one ever before him. Even though El Santo was the first major Luchador to achieve international fame, it was Mil Máscaras who traveled and became the crowd favorite in all his adopted hometowns. To this day, he still wrestles and routinely beats men more than half his age.

El Murciélago

There are so many Luchadores and enmascarados who did so much for the growth of Lucha that trying to name them, let alone remember them, would be a Herculean task. Hundreds of men have stepped into the Lucha ring, some with careers that last decades and others who have donned the wrestler's tights and mask for one night. Lucha Libre has had its share of unique individuals, but one of the great all-time eccentrics ever to enter an arena was El Murciélago. El Murciélago literally was on the ground floor of the temple that would become Lucha Libre.

He wasn't always known by such a macabre name. He was born Jesús Velázquez Quintero on October 30, 1909, in Guanajuato, and first spread his wings as El Murciélago Enmascarado (Masked Bat) against Jack O'Brien at Arena Mexico on April 3, 1938. His brawling, rough style got him disqualified in that match, but it set the dark tone for his style for years to come—and what a style! Part panache, part Grand Guignol, all show, he would come into the ring donned in all black. His hood, trunks and boots were completely black, and, as noted before, to make the gothic-like ensemble complete, he would carry a sack full of live bats and release them into the crowd before the match started. Genius! His style evolved from the tough, brawling mauler to a scientific ring technician. El Murciélago's evil aura grew into legendary infamy when he supposedly knocked the eye out of one of his opponents during a match. A myth grew out of this incident. Some people claim to have been in the arena that night and had seen it happen; others say that it never occurred, but it floated around so long it became like that line from *The Man Who Shot Liberty Valence:* "When the legend becomes fact, print the legend." Whether he knocked out Merced Gómez's eye that night or if the ex-boxer had eye damage before he stepped into the Lucha ring will always be up for contention, but El Murciélago chewed on that bone of notoriety and sucked out every ounce of press he could get. And if taking his eye wasn't enough, El Murciélago took the hair of rival Merced Gómez. El Murciélago wrestled in some of the very first máscara contra cabellera matches and scalped Bobby Bonales, Dientes Hernández, and Ciclón Veloz. The one máscaras contra cabellera match that would become epic was his battle with the highly stylized Octavio Gaona. On July 18, 1940, El Murciélago had his wings clipped; his famous black mask was removed, and this is considered the first unmasking of a major masked superstar in Lucha.

But what would have finished almost any other enmascarado's career was actually a new phase in El Murciélago's. He began again and fought some of the biggest marquee names in the business— always selling out wherever and whenever he wrestled in 1941. But soon El Murciélago heard the distant

BELOW: **A rare photo of Murciélago Velázquez: his style and colorful ways helped pave the way for men like Santo and Blue Demon**

OPPOSITE: **There was nothing angelic about** rudo Ángel Blanco

flutter of another pair of dark wings flying up the ranks of Lucha in the forties: a new masked wrestler (who had the audacity to name himself El Murciélago Enmascarado II) was on the scene. Well, El Murciélago was not pleased about the copycat upstart using his name, and he took his grievances to the Lucha commission. They found in his favor, and El Murciélago Enmascarado II was ordered to cease and desist using that famous name. By all accounts that young man did all right by his new name, El Santo.

El Murciélago wrestled into the fifties but by that time he was considered a little long in the tooth (or fang) and was no longer the top draw he had been earlier in his career. But the multitalented Murciélago didn't terrify fans in just the arenas, he did a pretty good job in the movie theaters as well. He became an actor, and in 1957 made his debut in *La Momia Azteca* (The Aztec Mummy). He also found some fame behind the camera as a screenwriter—the man of unbridled terror in the ring proved to be a well-rounded gentleman outside of it. Later in his life he became the Distrito Federal Lucha Libre commissioner and always kept his hand in the sport he loved so much. He divided his time between Lucha and film, writing various scripts in several different genres. By the early seventies there would be no more scripts or matches from El Murciélago. He quietly glided out of this world on May 26, 1972.

Ángel Blanco
(WHITE ANGEL)

Ángel Blanco's earthly identity was that of José Ángel Vargas Sánchez. He was born in the city of Atoyac, Jalisco State, on August 2, 1936, and like all young men aspired to step into the Lucha ring, José sought out the best trainers to help him develop into a top-notch Luchador. Under the watchful eyes of Miguel Navarrete and the fabled Diablo Velazco, the young José underwent the rigorous training regime to condition young men into hearty Luchadores. He started out first as a pro in the early sixties, debuting in Morelia, Michoacán, as "Ranchero" Vargas and his first opponent was Carlos Mayo. Soon after, he donned a mask and changed his persona to El Gato Negro (Black Cat) but

that turn as an enmascarado didn't last long. He lost his mask to José Gómez in Iraputo, Guanajuato.

The next incarnation for José was to be one half of Los Hermanos Diablo. His partner in that demonic duo was Black Gordman. He eventually evolved from satanic sibling to angelic superstar when Torreón promoter Gonzalo Gómez baptized him into the Lucha family as El Ángel Blanco. With a more heavenly sounding handle, he made his debut with tag team partner Goliath in the Plaza de Toros de Torreón in 1962. Soon after, El Ángel Blanco teamed up with another white-masked enmascarado, the famed Dr. Wagner, and this pairing created one of the more successful and devastating teams in Lucha history. Calling themselves La Ola Blanca (The White Wave), this pair of powerful rudos hit with a tsunami-like fury, punishing opponents under a storm of intensity rarely seen in arenas around Mexico. And if the powerful combination of El Ángel

Blanco and Dr. Wagner wasn't fearsome enough, it got even more formidable when another famous masked man joined their unit.

El Solitario became their partner in crime and the three of them wreaked havoc throughout the ranks of Lucha. But as the trio thrashed their opponents, El Solitario slowly started to slip away from the dark side of the rudo to gradually become a técnico—with the support of the crowds but to the chagrin of his partners. So what were El Ángel Blanco and Dr. Wagner to do with their estranged partner? What any self-respecting rudo would do: They gave him a tremendous beat down that resulted in some great matches for the fans and profitable outings for the promoters.

Ángel was a busy man during this time. Not only was he teaming up with Dr. Wagner to peter out punishment, he was apt at doing it by himself. He had a very competitive career as a singles competitor—waging great mano-a-mano feuds with the legendary Ray Mendoza and Dory Dixon. But the one feud that brought out the best (which is usually the worst in a rudo of Ángel's stature) was the heated battles he had with his former friend and ex-partner, El Solitario. That war came to a head on December 8, 1972, when both enmascarados faced each other in the most severe match that two men of that caliber could participate in, the dreaded máscara contra máscara.

SOLITARIO - ÁNGEL BLANCO

After a hard-fought battle during which fans screamed themselves raw, El Solitario came out victorious. Ángel had his angelic feathers plucked, his mask taken off and suddenly his true identity was known throughout the celestial world.

Now, most enmascarados who lost their mask usually lost some of the prestige that went with being a famed masked wrestler, but

Ángel's unmasking took a different turn. His intense demeanor and charismatic personality actually came out stronger when his mask was removed, like the famous El Murciélago years before. Ángel's career went the same route—gaining as much popularity as he had when he wore his feared white mask. He even got a new breath of fresh air blown into this new phase of his career when some fans and magazines went back to using his first Lucha name, "Ranchero" Vargas. An old name and a new beginning meant a successful start for Ángel's next outing as a Luchador. Ángel held various championship belts in his career, but as the grind of the Luchador lifestyle wore on him, he started slowing down, playing smaller arenas (but always as the main headliner). Then came the inevitable, his showdown with his former White Wave cohort Dr. Wagner. Both men were older than the first time they wrestled together, but their competitive fires had not diminished and their combative spirits still raged on.

But it was not in the cards for Ángel to wrestle for a few more years, then peacefully segue into a quiet retirement. On April 26, 1986, Ángel was coming back from a show in Nuevo Laredo, Tamaulipas. Riding along with him were fellow Luchadores Jungla Negra, Solar I, Mano Negra, and his old friend and foe Dr. Wagner. The car crashed, and the injuries suffered by Ángel led to his death. To further force the suffering by the world of Lucha, Dr. Wagner suffered serious neurological damage that left him in a wheelchair and out of the business he loved and fought so long in. One has to wonder what the mood of that car ride must have been before the accident, because less than three weeks earlier Ángel's and Wagner's former ally and adversary—El Solitario—lost his own life. In less than a month in 1986 Lucha Libre sustained a trio of devastating blows. The White Angel was now with the real ones in the heavens.

El Solitario

They say the good die young. If that is true then the great shuffle off this mortal coil all the sooner. That was the case with the enmascarado legend El Solitario. Born Roberto González Cruz on May 22, 1946, in Yahualica, a small town of Jalisco, the young Cruz grew up poor, in a large family where it was hard for even simple needs to be met.

The family struggled; Cruz's older brother, Jesús, wrestled under the name Othón Banzica in local arenas to earn money to take home to his family. But a tragic accident occurred in 1959 (one of many that would eventually plague Cruz during his too-short life) and Cruz's beloved brother Jesús was killed in the ring.

Cruz was devastated over the loss of his brother, something he never got over. Fueled with the anger of losing Jesús in such a strange and sad way, and despising his living situation, Cruz was desperate to get out. He knew there was more to life than his small town, backbreaking work, poverty and drudgery. He left home in his early teens and set out for a world that would bring him out of the despair he escaped from—the very same world his brother Jesús tried to reach and just missed. That brave new world was Lucha Libre.

Cruz was determined that he would succeed in Lucha Libre, and by proxy, so would his brother, whose spirit Cruz always believed guided him. Against his parents' frantic pleas, Cruz went away to train. He was determined to make it as a Luchador, and with the added help of his brother watching over him in heaven, he started training at the Gallo Madrugador Gym under trainer Joe El Hermoso. Cruz had a natural athletic ability, a strong will, and those two traits led Cruz to an extremely early debut in the Lucha Libre ranks when he was less than fifteen! Cruz wrestled for promoter Elías Simón and used several different gimmicks and names as a young, fresh-faced Luchador, but nothing sat well with the youngster until he changed his name to Othón Banzica II in honor of his fallen older brother.

ABOVE: El Solitario aka El Enmascarado de Oro (The Man of the Golden Mask) and Mil Máscaras (The Man of 1,000 Masks) teaming up in Japan

EL HALCON
AÑO DOCE - No. 590.
AGOSTO 21 DE
La Pareja de Seda y Oro
ANIBAL
Y EL
SOLITARIO

Cruz's heart and soul may have been firmly determined to make it in the wrestling world but he was still a teenager. Although he was athletic, he wasn't fully developed yet and was without the imposing physiques the other, older, Luchadores possessed. So the hardworking Cruz did the one thing he thought he should do—he worked harder. His endeavors paid off and people began to notice him—especially promoters Julián Sánchez and Ray Plata from Arena Coliseo in Guadalajara, Jalisco.

The newly hulking Cruz needed a new name and identity to separate him from his Othón Banzica II persona, simultaneously freeing him from the tragedy that befell his family. That came with the influence of famous TV character El Llanero Solitario (the Lone Ranger), which helped guide Cruz to his new identity—El Solitario. Not wanting to get into legal problems, Cruz thought it would be wise just to call himself El Solitario (The Lonely One), but the black design around the eyes of his mask still suspiciously resembled the Lone Ranger's famous mask.

With his new name he came on strong in 1966, participating in not one but two máscaras contra máscaras, beating and unmasking both Aguila Tapatía and The White Hand (La Mano Blanca) but that wasn't all—he fought in a máscara contra cabellera match against Luis González and took his hair along with his Occident Welterweight title.

El Solitario was on his way to becoming the "real" Legend Killer when he faced Ray Mendoza in another máscara contra cabellera; he defeated the legend, and scalped him on December 13, 1968. But not content to sit on a victory that would have been a major feather in any

Luchador's cap, in true rudo fashion he faced the famous René Gua-jardo, whom he beat and left bald in the ring. It looked like there would be no stopping this dangerous upstart, especially when he defeated El Rayo de Jalisco on August 15, 1969, to win the NWA World Middleweight title. Then two feared rudos noticed the aggressive and formidable El Solitario and decided he would be the perfect addition to their already unbeatable team. Ángel Blanco and Dr. Wagner—the tandem that was known as La Ola Blanca (The White Wave)—brought El Solitario under their treacherous wings.

But El Solitario was such a rising star that it wasn't long before jealousy reared its ugly head. The White Wave crashed down hard on Solitario when Ángel and the not-so-good Doctor turned the tables and ambushed their new partner. Solitario would have his revenge on the men who betrayed him. He quickly started a feud with Ángel, and on December 8, 1972, in one of the most highly anticipated máscara contra máscara in Lucha history, Solitario got his pound of flesh and then some when he defeated Ángel and took his mask.

With one double-crossing former ex-partner down, Solitario would have to remember that famous old Sicilian saying "revenge is a dish best served cold"—it took *fifteen years* for Solitario to get into the ring with the other half of the traitorous pair that turned on him. But when he did square off with Dr. Wagner the fans knew the outcome would be volcanic. On December 1, 1985, they faced off in an explosive máscara contra máscara match in a sold-out Plaza de Toros Monumental de Monterrey. For an event of this magnitude a special referee had to be brought in, a man who would be able to control the action in the ring as well as the dominant personalities behind the masks. That nod went to the famous Ray Mendoza, the same man who Solitario beat and scalped years earlier.

Even though Solitario had to wait years to get his shot at revenge at Dr. Wagner, he savored every second of it, and came out on top like he did years earlier against Ángel Blanco. Solitario unmasked Dr. Wagner for the world to see. After that, Solitario was on fire—and not just in Mexico. His popularity spread across the border into America and all the way to Japan. He won an impressive list of titles, matches and masks against some sterling competition. Many thought his career could have been one of the greatest in Lucha history. But the longevity that many Luchadores have enjoyed sadly eluded Solitario. On April 6, 1986, the masked Lonely One passed away at the age of thirty-nine. There have been many rumors circulating after his death, like most famous men that pass away too young; stories that cannot be substantiated have made the rumor circles around the Lucha Libre world. Officially, he had a heart attack and passed away while undergoing surgery for an injury. We'll leave it at that. His name does live on in his son; "El Hijo del Solitario" continues to carry on the Solitario name, but the legend of the Lonely One died on that operating table twenty years ago.

Dr. Wagner

On becoming a doctor one takes the Hippocratic oath, which states in no uncertain terms that a doctor shall do no harm to anyone. It seems that perhaps Dr. Wagner missed the day the oath was administered, because causing pain to his opponents was a full-time occupation for this man of medical mayhem. He began life on April 13, 1936, as Manuel González Rivera. Like so many others, the love of Lucha took hold of Rivera at a young age, and he found himself training for the ring at Gimnasio Hércules in Guadalajara. Rivera worked hard, not just in his training but also as a manual laborer so he could support himself and fund his dream (it might have been easier to go to real medical school).

BELOW: Why is this man smiling? Because he probably left a devastated opponent unconscious in the ring: The evil Dr. Wagner

After a few years of strenuous training he debuted on July 16, 1961, as the sinister-sounding Centella Negra (Black Lightning Spark), teaming with Torbellino Negro (Black Whirlwind). This dark-sounding duo's first match was against Pancho Ramírez and Monje Loco (Mad Monk). Promoter Elías Simón watched Rivera wrestle and knew an opportunity when he saw it. So on Simón's behest, Rivera went about changing his Centella Negra moniker to something that would resonate with the fans. A year earlier, famed and feared enmascarado

Médico Asesino had died. Fans always loved the idea of a rudo doctor wrestler, so it was suggested by Simón that Rivera become El Hijo del Médico Asesino (the Son of Médico Asesino). Rivera liked the idea of being a doctor but disliked carrying on the false lineage of the famous wrestler who passed away far too young. He decided on the name Dr. Wagner. (I asked a Mexican friend what "Dr. Wagner" might mean—did it have some sort of diabolical connotation? Does "Wagner" in Spanish stand for "brutal" or "maniacal"? My friend said, "No, Wagner means Wagner." So, it didn't have a menacing ring to it like Médico Asesino, but fans would find out soon enough that this man was no kindhearted country doctor.)

Rivera graduated from intimidating intern to a medical professional with a degree in devastation when he debuted as Dr. Wagner in the celebrated Arena Isabel in Cuernavaca. The first patient to be treated to his unconventional therapy was Rubén Juárez. It wasn't long before the Doctor's patient list grew very long. Wagner fought as a tag partner as well as a singles competitor and scored a major

MIL MÁSCARAS VS. DR. WAGNER SR. (1979)

win over crowd favorite Raúl "Moritas" Reyes on July 17, 1966, in a máscara contra cabellera match. The Doctor kept his mask and Moritas went home looking like Kojak. Wagner had attained super-star status, but that fortuitous streak would take an infamous turn later that year.

At times it seems that fate throws similarly evil-minded people together in such a random and bizarre fashion that the teaming of these certain nasty individuals is definitely bad for society but certainly beneficial to the two rogues who have become cohorts. It happened with the body snatchers Burke and Hare, it happened when Leopold hooked up with Loeb and it happened in 1966 when Dr. Wagner joined forces with an equally diabolical individual, El Ángel Blanco. Although they both possessed merciful-sounding names, they were far from compassionate when they stepped into the ring. In December 1966 "La Ola Blanca" defeated the famous team of El Santo and Rayo de Jalisco for the National Tag Team titles. The pair cemented their supremacy as "the" tag team to beat.

But Wagner had always been a successful wrestler on his own before teaming up with Ángel, and he kept proving this fact in singles competition. He won the National Light Heavyweight title on March 16, 1973, by beating Enrique Vera. Known by fans as El Galeno del Mal (The Evil Doctor), Wagner defended this title many times and against many opponents, but he had his sights on a bigger title. Wagner abdicated his throne and fought for the World title. After a grueling tournament, Wagner won the NWA World Light Heavyweight championship. He eventually lost his mask to Solitario.

Wagner kept working and wrestling all over Mexico, eventually slowing down his pace to give his body a rest and to help the fledgling career of his own son Dr. Wagner Jr. But tragedy struck in the same car accident that killed Ángel Blanco. This devastated Wagner both physically and emotionally; he always felt responsible for his beloved friend's death. After years of rehabilitation he was able to walk with a cane, and he opened up a gym to teach Luchadores and did help guide his sons, Dr. Wagner Jr. and Silver King, to successful careers. The final curtain came down on Wagner on September 12, 2004, when he passed away from a heart attack. He was sixty-eight.

Médico Asesino

The Medical Assassin was born Cesáreo Manríquez González. There is speculation about his real date of birth (how appropriate that his medical records would be suspect) but most experts agree that he was born August 27, 1920, in Chihuahua, Chihuahua. Cesáreo's first foray into the sport was that of a timekeeper when he worked for promoter Giraldo del Hierro at Palacio de los Deportes. He moved from watching the clock to watching the matches and became a referee. From there his natural size was an indicator that he would be more apt at administering pain than trying to control the action in the ring. He began wrestling as Don Cesáreo, but it was promoter Elías Simón who saw the potential in Cesáreo's ability and had him change his name to "El Asesino."

For a while he was called La Bestia and was gaining some momentum when his luck took a turn for the worse. On September 23, 1945, in a match against Rito Romero, he lost his mask in the Plaza de Toros el Progreso in Guadalajara, Jalisco. Becoming an unmasked enmascarado damaged his career, his popularity plummeted and for a while he found himself out of the Lucha world. But Cesáreo found himself missing the old lifestyle and he went to promoter Jesús "Chucho" Garza, whom he wrestled for in Monterrey, and told him he wanted back in. At this time Garza was making a deal to book some of his talent on Televicentro (which has become Televisa) and the concept of showing Lucha Libre matches across the country on television was going to revolutionize the business. Garza had Cesáreo come down to the station and before his first match on national TV, he christened him "El Médico Asesino."

Cesáreo's graduation present was a black medical bag, a white doctor's smock, a black mask and a license to commit mayhem. The doctor was open for business and his first house call was on February 9, 1952, when he teamed up with Wolf Ruvinskis to defeat the tough team of Tonina Jackson and Enrique Llanes. Médico Asesino's rough style and in-ring attitude made him a rudo people loved to hate.

Médico Asesino teamed up with some equally vicious partners in the fifties. He fought alongside men like Carnicero Butcher, El Espectro and El Bulldog, and his reputation grew as fans flocked to the television sets to get their weekly dose of the doctor. One of his signature moves was *castigo a las carótidas*—grabbing opponents by the neck, lifting them up and choking them out. It was a sight to see the massive doctor manhandling his opponents with such disregard. He is credited as being the first progressive-minded enmascarado to bring a sexy female attendant to the ring. This hot valet was named La Enfermera del Médico Asesino, but the people weren't as savvy as they are today and they didn't see back then what is a staple in wrestling now—the combo of sex and violence sells.

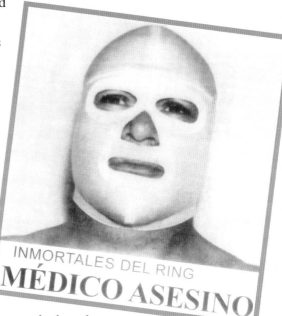

INMORTALES DEL RING
MÉDICO ASESINO

ABOVE: **Médico Asesino, one of the first and greatest rudos of Lucha Libre**

Luscious women and virile wrestlers cater to the demographics that watch and appreciate wrestling. Back then Lucha events were still attended by people wearing suits and ties. Even though unbridled violence was anticipated and cheered, it seemed that any attention of overt sexuality was frowned upon most likely because of the strict sense of decorum brought on by centuries of Catholic dominance.

Médico Asesino was on a roll, crowds booed him, TV fans watched him, but everyone's attention was on him, and in the wrestling business it is better to be hated by everyone than to be loved by a few. Mayor Ernesto P. Uruchurtu of Mexico City banned wrestling from the airwaves so the Médico Asesino was off TV but he was still a fan favorite. Top promoter and top talent culminated in an epic battle on April 27, 1956, at the grand opening of the newly rebuilt Arena Mexico, where Médico Asesino and his partner El Santo fought Rolando Vera and Blue Demon in one of the most brutal matches in history. Médico Asesino was a big man and on those broad shoulders EMLL decided to carry the defunct Heavyweight division (unlike American wrestling, where only the big men get noticed, Lucha Libre is more akin to boxing with all its weight divisions getting a fair shake).

VELAZQUEZ   ARMANDO SILVES

H CAMPBELL   •   ROBERTO CAÑED

FANTE   CHUCHO SALINA

HADORAS EN   en

LTOS DE LUCHA LIBRE

DORAS VS.   CON LOS LUCHADORES:
MURCIELAGO VELAZ
CAVERNARIO GALIN
Y LAS SALVAJES LUCHADOR
ASESINO   CHABELA ROMERO
(INTERPRETANDO "VENDETTA
MARTHA "GÜERA" S
MAGDALENA CABALL

His stature as one of the top guys in the business was secure, but the strong and formidable Médico began to fall ill in the late fifties. His once intimidating physique and menacing ring presence started to slowly diminish. On June 16, 1960, he died of cancer, leaving a legacy that for many today is largely forgotten except for those who knew him, saw him wrestle, and wrestled with him or against him. They will never forget the white-masked man who terrorized and popularized the Lucha Libre world in its Golden Age.

Huracán Ramírez

Daniel García came from a family that was deeply entrenched in Lucha Libre; all three of his brothers, La Pantera Roja, Ruddy García, and El Demonio Rojo, were Luchadores. But even though Lucha ran in their bloodlines, García's brothers wanted him to pursue a safer athletic endeavor, and he chose boxing. He boxed during the forties under his real name, but by 1952 he jumped ship and followed in his brothers' footsteps. He debuted as a rudo, El Buitre Blanco (The White Vulture) but at this time the character Huracán Ramírez appeared on the silver screen in a movie named *Huracán Ramírez.* In the series of films that the character Huracán Ramírez would star in, an actor would portray the unmasked true identity of Huracán Ramírez, but when that character donned his mask to fight evil, a real Luchador played him.

The first guy to play Huracán on the screen was Spanish wrestler Eduardo Bonada, but after his film debut he thought he was too good-looking to have his face covered

up and he left the series. A litany of Luchadores were hot for the Huracán role, but with so many individuals playing Huracán there was definitely some confusion going on. The idea was to find one man to be Huracán on the screen and in the ring. They needed consistency if they were going to keep their successful franchise character going strong and if the in-ring incarnation was going to make it in the real world of Lucha Libre and not just the fake one in the movies.

García had already had smaller roles in some of the Huracán films and he was handed the whole shebang. Daniel García became Huracán Ramírez on screen and in the ring. During his career he took the masks of some top enmascarados in the game: Halcón de Oro, Moloch, Espanto III, The Scorpio, El Enfermero, Cadaver II, La Sombra, and he teamed up with Rayo de Jalisco to collect the masks of Los Hermanos Muerte. He collected a few championships along the way; he won the NWA World Welterweight title from Karloff Lagarde, the National Welterweight title three times, and the Northern Middleweight title. One of the most enduring things about his career was a maneuver that would become his signature move and is still used today with devastating results. When someone does the Huracánrana, it is a nod to the original Huracán. And the name is still carried on today by his nephew Huracán Jr.

Tinieblas

Although his name means "darkness" there is nothing gloomy about the successful career of Tinieblas. His career in a way resembles that of Huracán Ramírez and Mil Máscaras—his character's persona was thought of before there was a man to fill that suit and mask, but the man who did fill it has kept it running strong and popular for years. Such a mystery surrounds this man in the faceless black mask that even his name has never been openly revealed to the public and the legend of his birth fluctuates between 1939 and 1945. He truly lived up to his name by keeping everyone in the dark with regard to who he really was. Most people in the know believe the man behind the dark façade was actually named Manuel Leal.

It is known that magazine editor Valente Pérez, the same man who invented the character Mil Máscaras and then discovered the man to become Mil Máscaras, was working on another project, creating an enmascarado who possessed the complete opposite traits that his hero Mil had. He would create an arch nemesis and give Mil someone with whom to feud; that is how Tinieblas was born. He was supposed to represent the darkness in all of us. He would become Mil Máscaras's evil alter ego. But even though he was conceived to be evil, Tinieblas became a técnico.

In his first match on August 20, 1971, he was pitted against one of the more formidable groups around, the trio of Dr. Wagner, El Solitario and Renato Torres. The men on his side were just as rough as the roughest rudos around, the two men that first discovered him: The Black Shadow and Dory Dixon. Tinieblas never disappointed them or the fans. Tinieblas also became a sensation in the pages of the comics and became one of the all-time favorite comic book characters ever in Mexico. He has wrestled all over and for various promotions—EMLL, AAA, Promo Azteca—and his son Tinieblas Jr. followed his dad's dark steps into the ring. Tinieblas also has a little mascot to accompany him to the ring, Alushe—a cross between an ewok and a squirrel with a thyroid condition; he is a furry little sidekick portrayed by a midget.

La Parka

La Parka is Adolfo Tapia Ibarra and he was born November 14, 1965, in Torreón, Coahuila. Adolfo started wrestling in the early eighties but his career really took off in 1992 when he donned a black skeleton costume. The design is very reminiscent of the Italian comic book character Kriminal crossed with He-Man's nemesis Skeletor. He teamed many times with Psicosis and had long-running feuds with Lizmark and Konnan. In 1994 he wrestled in *When Worlds Collide*, the joint AAA/WCW pay-per-view special. From there he spent a

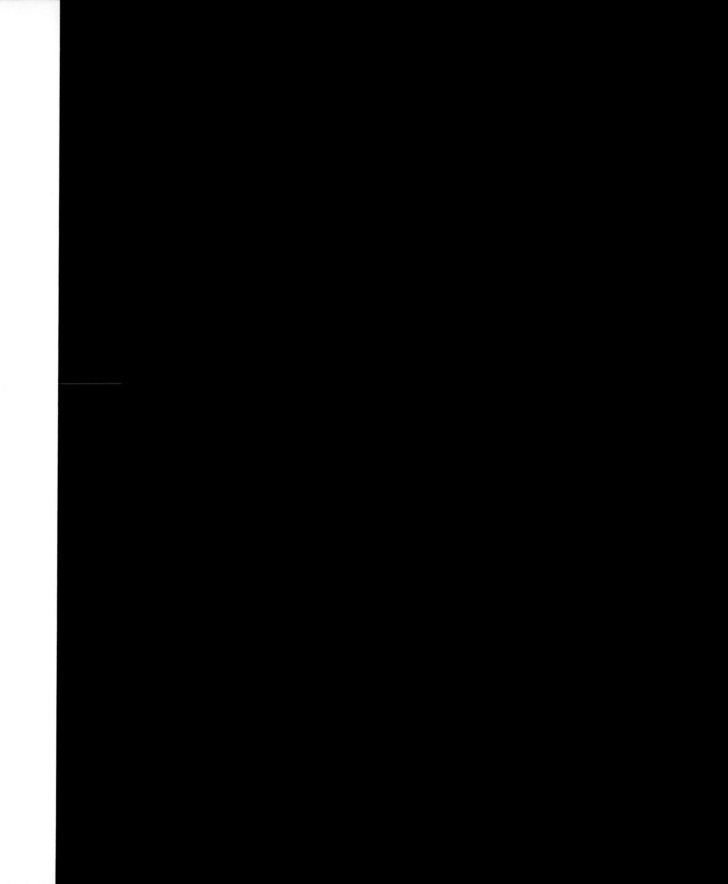

short time in Heyman's ECW promotion. Later, he went to work for WCW (World Championship Wrestling) and took on the nickname "The Chairman of the Board," where his gimmick was to hit his opponents with a chair.

There is some controversy today about who is the *real* La Parka. Long story short, here is the inside skinny. Ibarra left AAA and went to work for rival CMLL, but he did not have the rights to his ring name. Antonio Peña, the head booker for AAA, kept the original La Parka moniker, so Ibarra changed his ring name to L. A. Park. To add some more confusion into the La Parka story, another Luchador (Jesús Alfonso Escoboza) donned a skeletal mask and took over the La Parka mystique for Peña's organization. Confused yet? It gets better. Ibarra's uncle, the Luchador formerly known as Volador, became "Super Parka." He wears a red skeleton custome with the big red "S" on his chest (and *privates*). So there it is, two men with practically the same ring name, give or take a vowel, but one works for AAA (Escoboza) and the original (Ibarra) works for CMLL. Purists consider Ibarra the only true La Parka in Lucha today.

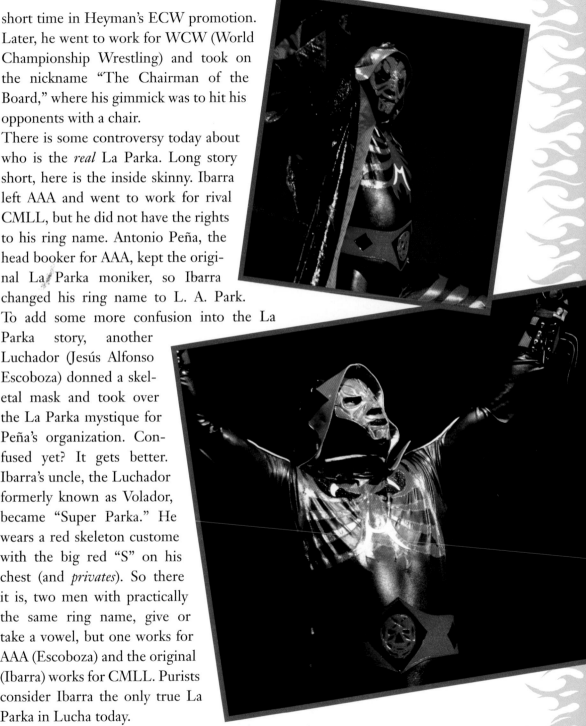

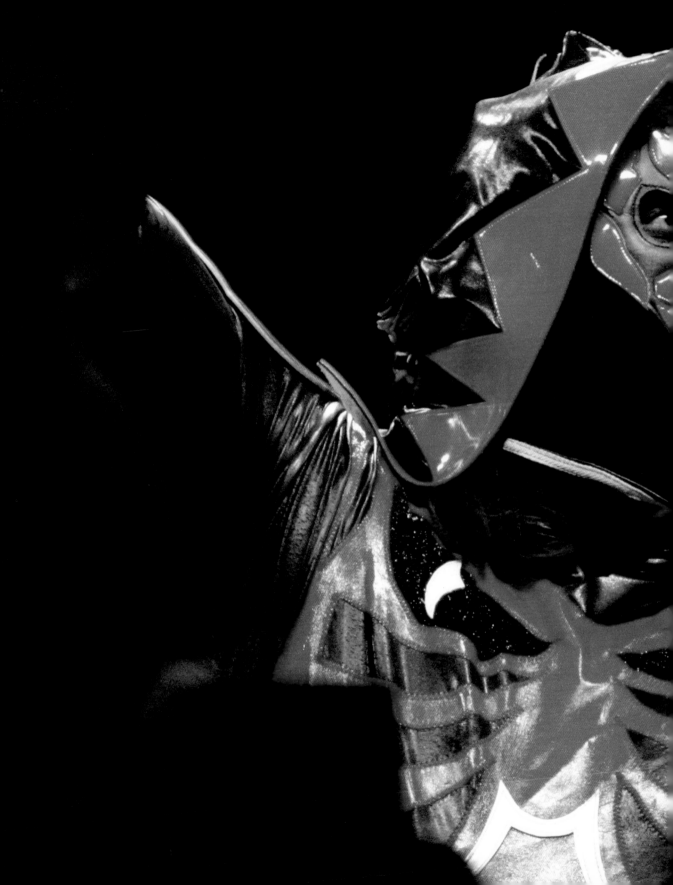

ABOVE: A red-masked
La Parka stands next
to Máscara Sagrada

El Hijo del Santo

It must be hard for children to grow up in the shadow of a famous parent. For youngsters living with fame all around them, can you blame them for wanting to step in the family footsteps and carry on the tradition that garnered all that glory? In Lucha Libre it is almost expected for sons to follow their fathers into the ring. Some sons eclipse their forefather's careers, and some sons are born into a legacy that is impossible to break out of. That is the case of El Hijo del Santo (The Son of the Saint). No other son had so many eyes looking at him when he decided to follow his legendary father into the ring. His father wasn't just a Luchador or an enmascarado, he was El Santo. He was known throughout the world by multitudes of fans and by millions who had never seen or heard of Lucha Libre but knew the image of "the Man with the Silver Mask." He was a cross-cultural icon. To be his son and to want to carry on in the family business must have been an unbearable burden to carry. But that is just what El Hijo del Santo did.

Even though his famous father didn't want his son to go into Lucha without a college degree behind him, El Hijo went into the ring. He started wrestling in February 1982, not as El Hijo del Santo but as "El Korak," he didn't have his father's permission and blessing yet to wrestle and it wasn't until the old man said "college first, the ring second" that El Hijo finally changed his ring name to that which echoes his father's legendary moniker, "El Hijo del Santo." He did receive his college degree in Communication Science, so he made his father happy and proud. El Hijo is one of eleven children Santo had (with two wives) and he is the only child who has wanted to emulate his father and go into the ring.

OPPOSITE: Red-robed El Hijo del Santo enters the ring for battle

ABOVE: Like father like son, El Hijo del Santo giving it his all

BELOW: The most prized possession in all of Lucha Libre, your opponent's *máscara*

OPPOSITE: Second-generation rivals El Hijo del Santo stretches out Scorpio Jr. in a *máscara contra cabellera* (mask vs. hair) match

From the moment he stepped in the ring, critics and fans and skeptics all scrutinized El Hijo's in-ring abilities. But like any other enmascarado starting out, he had to pay his dues. Just because your father is famous doesn't mean that talent is hereditary. El Hijo wrestled in small venues at first and worked for the Tijuana circuit and then moved up to UWA, but once again the eyes of Consejo Mundial de Lucha Libre were on the Santo name and brought up the young man and were not disappointed. Not only was he an immediate crowd favorite, he won Rookie of the Year in 1983. And like his father, he had his sights set on a *campeonato* (championship). That came in October 1985 when he won the UWA World Lightweight title from Aristóteles. He held on to that title until 1988 when an old nemesis of the family took it from him, Espanto Jr. (the original Espanto, his father, was

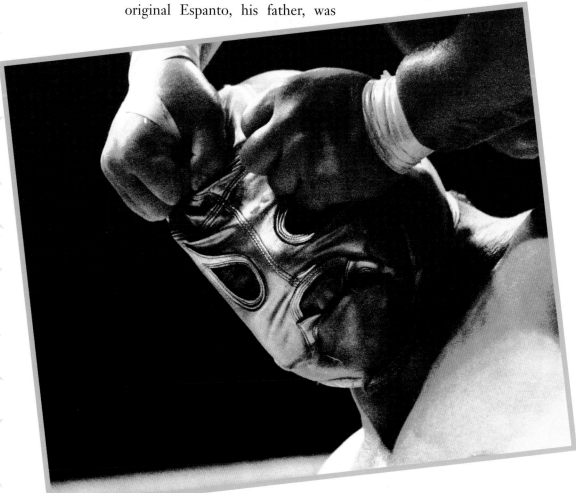

a rival of El Santo; this was a second-generation grudge match). El Hijo had some bitter battles with Espanto Jr. and won his title back as well as Espanto Jr.'s mask in one match and his hair in another. In 1990 he won the UWA Welterweight title but left that promotion and went to work for Asistencia Asesoría y Administración (AAA).

Then came another second-generation matchup. This time El Hijo was battling his dad's former friend and partner's son, Eddie Guerrero. Guerrero and Art "Love Machine" Barr faced El Hijo del Santo and his partner Octagón at *When Worlds Collide* pay-per-view. Since then, El Hijo del Santo has feuded with some of the biggest names of his generation, Negro Casas, Scorpio Jr., El Dandy, Villano III, Fuerza Guerrera, Bestia Salvaje, Perro Aguayo Jr., Los Guerreros del Infierno ("The Warriors from Hell" duo of Último Guerrero and Rey Bucanero), and has taken the masks of some rough customers: Aristóteles I, Cosmonauta, El Diluvio, La Momia, El Galáctico, El Buitre, El Pierroth, Aristóteles II, El Ninja, Skeletor, Kato Kung Lee, Silver King, León Chino, Starman, Guerrero del Futuro, El Nuevo Huracán Ramírez Jr., Dr. Cerebro, El Hijo del Cobarde, Vikingo del Futuro, and Super Parka. He has won some pretty prestigious titles along the way.

El Hijo's career stands on its own now. For his generation and the next generations he will be the Santo. Still wrestling around Mexico and all over the world, El Hijo del Santo has proudly kept the family name alive in the hearts of Lucha fans everywhere.

RIGHT: Bloodied and beaten but unbowed: the Son of Santo rises to victory after taking a hellacious beat-down

6

The Biz

LUCHA LIBRE *is a business, and as such, promoters have been an integral part of the game; some call them a necessary evil. Good, bad, evil or benevolent—it doesn't matter. It must be understood: Without promoters there would be no wrestling business. Although the ranks of Lucha are filled with superstars and great Luchadores, someone put up the money to pay these athletes. Now, whether you like or dislike the promoter, it doesn't matter; if you're a Luchador the things that matter are these: Is he or she going to pay me (on time and in full)? Can he or she get me work and give me exposure? Forget about insurance or a union, Luchadores are independent contractors;*

OPPOSITE: U.F.E.: unidentified flying enmascarado in Mexico City ABOVE: If you're squeamish about the sight of blood, think twice about sitting ringside

their expenses come out of their pockets. The top names have deals worked out for them, but for the average wrestler working his behind off, it is a tough road to travel.

I have known a few promoters in both Lucha Libre and American professional wrestling, and like all walks of life, some are decent human beings trying to get along in life and others, well, the less said the better. I have spoken to Luchadores who had traveled very far to wrestle for very low money, only to be stiffed at the end of the night when an unscrupulous promoter vanished without paying up.

It happens in America, it happens in Mexico. After talking to a few of the decent, honest promoters (usually the smaller independent ones), I understand it takes a lot of money to run a Lucha show—they have to rent the hall, the ring, the chairs, pay for lights, security, advertising and some promoters even pay for travel and rooms, but that is not always the case. Some promoters will help with hospital or medical bills, plus the dozens of other little things that all add up in the end. And, of course, they have to pay the performers. It is not an easy life being a promoter, unless you are at the top of the business. All the local promoters I have met have other jobs to support them.

When Don Salvador Lutteroth laid down the Lucha Libre business plan some seventy years ago, it was a good blueprint to work from. He had looked over at his European counterparts across the sea, and at his North American rivals in the United States. He took what worked and tossed out what didn't. Lutteroth was the mainstay of Lucha Libre promotion for years. His promotion was originally known as Empresa Mexicana de la Lucha Libre (EMLL). It was in the EMLL that Luchadores got national exposure; it was the big league. El Santo, Blue Demon, Bobby Bonales, Tarzán Lopez, Gory Guerrero and countless other Luchadores and enmascarados got their starts in EMLL. "La

LUCHA IN THE '80s AND THE DEMISE OF THE MASKED MEXICAN WRESTLER IN AMERICA

by Ranjan Chhibber, PhD

rom the height of Mil Máscaras's main event at Madison Square Garden against WWF champion Superstar Billy Graham in the '70s, the Luchador (especially the enmascarado) underwent a vanishing act in the '80s in the WWF. It was the one era when Americans, outside of those in the Latino culture, never would have heard of a Lucha Libre. It was gone, eliminated from popular memory, and shelved under "ethnic interests" during the decade of greed.

The WWE (formerly the WWF) certainly could not be called anti-Latino in the '70s: After all, it made the legendary Pedro Morales a champ in the '70s; and then the technically savvy Tito Santana into one of its most respected Intercontinental Champions.

The WWWF's use of the mask was diametrically opposed to Lucha Libre's use of the mask: Where the Mexican mask holds an almost sacred power, in today's WWE, it connotes something more akin to a clown, or the Hamburglar.

Executing the Masked Wrestler

A telling example of how the masked wrestler was used in the WWF in the '80s is to look at its character "The Executioner." The Executioner was a clearly overweight wrestler whose body was way past its prime. His perennial losses would classify him as a "jobber" in wrestling terminology: someone who always loses a match. Jobbers are wonderful characters in their own right, but the Executioner was on the lower rung of even those pariahs of professional wrestling.

The Executioner was a joke, and treated as such. On an episode of *Tuesday Night Titans*, the "worked" wrestling terminology for "staged" or "scripted" talk show hosted and produced by Vince McMahon, McMahon interviewed the Executioner. The interview revealed the Executioner to be a bitter-sounding man who thought he was greater than he actually was. McMahon finally asked the million-dollar question: Why did the Executioner wear a mask?

Because no matter how athletic the Luchadores were, no matter how death-defying their moves, the top '80s American promotions did not respect the masked wrestlers. If you wore a mask in America in the "me" decade, you were just like the Executioner. Masked Luchadores faced an impossible choice if they wanted to wrestle in American promotions: to wrestle masked and be relegated to jobber status, or to lose their precious masks and sacrifice their Mexican careers for the small chance of becoming a star in America.

Hulk Hogan—'80s Enmascarado?

With no major American promoter putting his money behind developing a masked wrestler, the mask was used to mock other countries that used them. One of the most famous examples of this was the WWF storyline that centered around an allegedly famous tag team from Japan, the Machines. This storyline began when the late, great Andre the Giant was "suspended" from the WWF in a worked storyline to cover up serious surgery that Andre required. His main nemesis, manager Bobby "The Brain" Heenan, delighted in the suspension of the wrestler that caused his stable of wrestlers much grief in the ring.

But not long after the suspension of Andre, the new tag team of "The Machines" made its premiere in the WWF. Comprised of "The Super Machine" and "The Big Machine," they were masked wrestlers purported to be from Japan, but also international superstars with a large fan base in Mexico. They were men who seemed to have too-large girths to be Japanese masked wrestlers, and whose Japanese seemed to be limited to saying "Hi" when interviewed by Mean Gene Okerlund. If that wasn't suspect enough, a new Machine made his premiere: "The Giant Machine." Standing at 7'5" and saying "Hi" with a French accent, it was no secret that this was Andre the Giant using the mask when he became bored with the worked "suspension."

What is important to note is that the Machines were portrayed as being from Japan, yet also for being popular in Mexico. Both countries had a rich tradition of enmascarados, however, for those familiar with Lucha Libre's use of masks and their larger-than-life characters, the Machines seemed to be parodies at best, and a mockery at worst.

The Machines had a special Machine who made an appearance in a few shows. He was the most heavily muscled of the Machines, with a tanned body and gargantuan arms. He had a very gruff voice when he spoke. His name: The Hulk Machine. Clear to everyone that it was Hulk Hogan, the whole angle was revealed to be little more than a comedy skit. While the 1980s had a great number of masked Luchadores who could have been superstars in the WWF, promoters decided to make the Hulk Machine its most famous "Luchador."

Mask Confusion

Masks were also used as gimmicks meant to confuse referees in the '80s. One of the most famous use of masks in this regard came when the WWF gave them to an underrated but talented tag team known as The Killer Bees. However, they did not wear the masks to the ring. Nor did they wear them in promos. When did they wear their masks? They would put on their masks to confuse the referee. While masked, if one Killer Bee was injured during the match and too far to make a tag, when the referee's back was turned the other masked Killer Bee would slide in and take his injured opponent's place. The referee, none the wiser, would continue the match. The great announcer Gorilla Monsoon called this move "Mask Confusion," and it led the Killer Bees to many more victories.

The mistreatment of the mask in Killer Bee gimmicks speaks volumes: In Lucha Libre, the wrestler's mask could only be removed, as already pointed out earlier in this book, in the most important "mask versus mask" matches, where the loser would lose all that made him mystical and nearly holy, while the victor would take the mask of the vanquished and add it to his power. To the American promotions, the mask was simply a prop, not an icon—how could a masked Luchador ever wrestle in America in the '80s?

The End of the Luchador in Reagan's America: The Conquistadors

Perhaps nothing better exemplified the erasure of the Luchador than the late '80s WWF tag team, The Conquista dors. The Conquistadors were Jose Estrada and Jose Luis Rivera, two jobbers known to WWF viewers in the '80s. If you saw them in a match, it was virtually guaranteed that they would lose.

Like the Machines, they were presented as South American superstars with many championships in their illustrious career, but they maintained a sterling record of defeat in the WWF. This was the WWF's attempt to bury Lucha Libre: For viewers who had never seen the real thing, they would buy this worked history of the Conquistadors as the purported legitimate stars from Mexico. And if the Conquistadors always lost, then what was the point of even watching Lucha Libre? Sure, they had colorful costumes and masks, but so what? The Conquistadors were a joke, meant to be laughed at.

The end of the '80s saw the near erasure of ethnic wrestlers in the WWF. Unless the ethnic group was an opponent of America, like a Russian or an Iranian wrestler, the ethnic wrestler of the '80s was encouraged to assimilate into America's famed melting pot (with the rare exception of The British Bulldogs). Those who could not shed their ethnicity were turned into jobbers.

By the end of the '80s American wrestling was just that: American. Other than those who sought out or came upon Lucha Libre promotions, American and Canadian wrestling fans of the WWF, growing up in the '80s, would never have known a thing about Mil Máscaras or other great Luchadores.

The Cold War was at its height and you were either with the side of freedom or on the side of the Evil Empire. And to be on the side of freedom, you had to be American. Every country on America's side emulated America: dancing to American music, wearing American clothes, and trying to become Americans within their own countries. Wrestling, always a mirror of society, reflected this trend when the brilliant Canadian tag team the Fabulous Rougeau Brothers were repackaged as American wannabes, coming out to the catchy theme music "All American Boys" while carrying little flags of Old Glory. The Luchador who refused this brand of adoration and assimilation really didn't have a chance in Reagan's America.

The '90s probably would have been similar for the un abashed ethnic wrestler (including the Luchador) in the world of American professional wrestling, if it were not for one visionary genius—a man whose whole existence has been dedicated to giving the finger to popular attitudes in order to shape new ones. It was this man who gave Luchadores, including the dreaded masked variety, their biggest opportunity in American wrestling history. He was criticized for pushing financially risky ideas in his wrestling promotion. But that suited a man known to the world as Paul E. Dangerously just fine. ☠

Empresa" was the place to be for the next fifty years of Lucha Libre promotion. After decades of being known as EMLL, it changed its name to Consejo Mundial de Lucha Libre (CMLL). Sometimes CMLL is still referred to by its previous name. But no matter what it is called, it is the oldest Lucha Libre promotion still in existence.

In the 1970s, the constant struggle to keep the CMLL strong and fresh was a strain on Lutteroth. He left the company in the hands of his son, Chavo, and took a long deserved rest away from the sport he had cultivated. But once the senior Lutteroth was no longer at the helm of CMLL it began to weaken. Lucha icon and legend Ray Mendoza, who was one of the company's top bookers, along with a few other promoters, broke off from CMLL and formed the Universal Wrestling Association. UWA ran in Mexico City and in nearby Naucalpan against CMLL; they also took some of EMLL's younger Luchadores with them. UWA would be a force to reckon with for well over a decade, but due to a decreasing talent roster, bad business practices and another rival threat, it ceased to exist in the 1990s.

In the seventies, EMLL joined the National Wrestling Alliance as its Mexican affiliate, calling itself NWA-EMLL. The NWA was a group of independent professional wrestling promotions in North America that had been unified and in operation since the late 1940s. Before the 1980s, the NWA was the governing body for professional wrestling and ran the old "territory" system that allowed certain promoters to control different regions of the country. As long as

RIGHT: This flying dive outside the ring is called *suicida:* a flashy name for a dangerous move

promoters worked in a somewhat harmonious relationship and allowed bigger-named talents to be loaned out to their fellow promoters across the country, things would continue to prosper. But that wasn't the case. With the national expansion of the WWF (now the WWE), EMLL decided to pull up stakes and walk away from the dirty politics and chicanery that would soon follow between rival North American promoters. It was in the 1980s, when EMLL cut ties with the NWA, that EMLL changed its name to Consejo Mundial de Lucha Libre (CMLL).

Just as it looked like CMLL (EMLL) would miss the fallout of the NWA quagmire that was about to happen, they had their own disruption within the ranks. Longtime booker Antonio Peña broke away from the newly renamed CMLL and formed his own promotion, Asistencia Asesoría y Administración (AAA), in 1992, along with wrestler superstar Konnan (Cuban-born muscle man Charles Ashenoff). Just as Ray Mendoza did before him, Peña took much of the young talent with him when he jumped ship. Peña also left CMLL with a roster of middle-aged Luchadores, some past their physical prime, and the company's overall future looked dim. AAA began to look for talent from other Lucha venues.

It was in Tijuana that Peña saw two young enmascarados; he quickly signed Rey Mysterio Jr. and Psicosis. AAA soon exploded with top stars like El Hijo del Santo, Octagón, Blue Panther, the Casas brothers, Cien Caras, Perro Aguayo, Los Gringos Locos (the team of Eddie Guerrero, "Love Machine" Art Barr and "Madonna's Boyfriend" Louie Spicoli). Los Gringos Locos were the most hated group in Lucha Libre for their short run; in a sadly ironic twist of fate, all three Gringos passed away before the age of forty. AAA's rising popularity soon caused rival Ray Mendoza's Universal Wrestling Association (UWA) to pack it in. Peña was not going to let top UWA talent draws like Canek, Dos Caras and Los Villanos sit idle for long, and he signed them under the AAA banner.

With an implied fresher look and new angle on Lucha Libre, AAA took over the reigns for several years as the hot place for Lucha Libre promotions. They began promoting cards throughout Mexico,

ABOVE: Since the beginning, the *máscara* has undergone various changes and styles, each reflecting the man wearing it

usually going to out-of-the-way suburban areas or cities that didn't have regular promoters. AAA (or sometimes known as Promociones Antonio Peña [PAP]) brought Lucha to the fans.

AAA's popularity peaked with a co-promoted pay-per-view deal with North American WCW called *When Worlds Collide*, which was televised in the United States in 1994. But the golden age that was expected for AAA never materialized as planned. Shortly after the show, Art Barr, a founding member of Los Gringos Locos, died. Soon the grieving Eddie Guerrero and Louie Spicoli, the other two members of Los Gringos Locos, left the promotion. El Hijo del Santo left due to backstage creative disagreements. When the Mexican economy started to falter in the mid-1990s, AAA realized

MONDO LUCHA A GO-GO **141**

their pockets were not as deep as their rival CMLL's. They scaled back on their talent and promotions and tried to ride out the economic downfall. Lucha superstars Fuerza Guerrera and Blue Panther left when they saw that the economy began to show signs of trouble and AAA couldn't offer as much work to its stable of Luchadores. Fuerza and Panther tried their hand at their own organization by starting the independent promotion PROMELL. Taking some of the other AAA talent that wasn't happy, they became another promotion to deal with, and PROMELL eventually became Promo Azteca.

CMLL was not going to stand by and idly watch as their promotion began to dwindle. They began rebuilding and bringing named Luchadores back onto the roster. Using the now famous El Hijo del Santo vs. Negro Casas feud, CMLL once again became the flagship of Lucha Libre in Mexico. AAA still promotes Lucha Libre matches and regularly sells out big arenas like the legendary Toreo de Cuatro and continually tries to draw new talent to its roster. Meanwhile, CMLL has reclaimed its spot as the *numero uno* promotion. To this day, its weekly wrestling shows at the legendary Arena Mexico draw crowds of over 10,000 fans. Even though CMLL is the biggest promotion in the world it also tends to be the most conservative. The overly bloody matches that have been a mainstay in Lucha Libre are not televised, an inducement to attend live matches as many of the fans seem to thrive on the visceral experience.

Today CMLL is broadcast regularly on Televisa in Mexico, Galavisión in the United States and Telelatino in Canada. CMLL is now affiliated with New Japan Pro Wrestling, founded by legendary Japanese wrestler Antonio Inoki in 1972, and has an off-shoot promotion, CMLL Japan. For years Japanese promotions have sent their prospects to Mexico to work and train, not unlike a finishing school. Mexico has in return sent many of its own sons over to the Land of the Rising Sun. Just as Mexico and Spain had an open trade policy with each other when it came to sharing styles, techniques and training regimes in the thirties, Japan and Mexico now have the same type of cooperative working relationship between sister promotions.

PAUL HEYMAN: MESSIAH OF THE LUCHADORES

by Ranjan Chhibber, PhD

The 1990s arrived. American professional wrestling looked generally the same: Hulk Hogan was still winning championships in the WWF, Ric Flair was still winning championships in the newly solidified WCW and there were still no Luchadores making a splash in either organization. Lucha Libre had continued to flourish outside of America, but it had become irrelevant to mainstream American pop culture (and the countries that emulated it).

The masked wrestlers continued to be a joke . . . quite literally with the creation of Doink the Clown in 1993. Doink was an evil clown whose gimmick was playing cruel pranks, and the biggest prank the WWF played was on the enmascarados, whom Doink's mask ridiculed.

WCW decided to try to experiment from time to time, especially when new vice president Eric Bischoff took over the reins of the company. One of Bischoff's first acts was to present *When Worlds Collide* pay-per-view with the AAA promotion. For one night only, American wrestling fans could see the stars of Lucha Libre on a mainstream American wrestling show, including masked wrestlers who were not jobbers or clowns. But the WCW didn't like using these high-flying wrestlers in their company. American wrestling was American wrestling, Mexican wrestling was Mexican wrestling, and never the twain could meet, according to the WCW at the time. However, *When Worlds Collide* caught the eye of the owner of a new upstart American wrestling promotion, Extreme Championship Wrestling.

The Fallout of *When Worlds Collide*

Paul Heyman, also known as Paul E. Dangerously, wrested control of ECW from its previous owner and made it a venue for the most original and trendsetting wrestling seen in the U.S. in many decades. The first major change was to internationalize it again: He first brought over the hard-core Japanese puroresu style of wrestling to ECW, being influenced greatly by the Japanese Frontier Martial-Arts Wrestling (FMW) promotion led by Atsushi Onita. This wrestling was extremely bloody and violent, with flaming table matches, barbed wire matches and other gory affairs that had all but been eradicated in the WWF and WCW.

WCW's *When Worlds Collide* was also important to the history of Heyman's ECW, and to the history of Luchadores in America. First, Heyman sued WCW for copyright infringement since his ECW had promoted a show called *When Worlds Collide* on May 14, 1994. WCW's version didn't occur until November 1994. Heyman was able to cut a deal or two utilizing WCW wrestlers in his ECW shows, as part of the out-of-court settlement, thereby giving his promotion some more mainstream American wrestling talent.

More importantly, Heyman paid close attention to what exactly WCW's *When Worlds Collide* was all about. When he saw what Luchadores had to offer, he decided right there and then that he had to have them as part of ECW. One of many examples of his prescience, he foresaw that these hardworking enmascarados and Luchadores would be superstars.

Heyman understood the psychology and legacy of the masks in Lucha Libre, and he proved this just prior to his hiring of the Luchadores. In late 1994, he hired wrestler Matt Borne, who was the original Doink the Clown. Heyman had his announcer Joey Styles ridicule Doink and, more importantly, the promotion that created Doink, the WWF.

In subsequent weeks, Matt Borne was given the name "Borne Again," playing himself as a washed-up wrestler driven insane because of the Doink the Clown gimmick handed to him. In a tactic that has not been seen in Lucha Libre, Matt Borne would forcibly put his clown mask on the faces of his fallen opponents, a reversal of the idea that the mask is an icon of honor. In a stroke of brilliance, Heyman showed just how disrespectful the WWF's Doink gimmick was to enmascarados. Borne Again wanted to get rid of that mask, and no one else wanted it. Borne would say in his promos, "Feel my pain by wearing that mask."

A few months after WCW's *When Worlds Collide*, Heyman brought these underappreciated stars to the ranks of ECW.

Directly from that pay-per-view, he brought Rey Mysterio Jr., Eddie Guerrero, Psicosis, Chris Benoit (who wrestled as the masked Pegasus Kid overseas), and 2 Cold Scorpio in 1995, and later, La Parka and Juventud Guerrera, two talented enmascarados.

All of the above wrestlers were anathema to anything the two big promotions were interested in: They were smaller statured, foreign in most cases and focused upon an acrobatic, high-flying style of wrestling. Most importantly, some of these wrestlers wore masks; yes, the same masks that the WWF felt were unmarketable and an anachronism to modern wrestling booking. Heyman took a big risk bringing these Lucha Libre stars to his promotion, since American wrestling fans had not seen them in their own mainstream promotions for at least a decade. First, he arranged for their work visas so that they were able to wrestle in ECW on a regular basis, getting national exposure on ECW's syndicated show.

The importance of the visa issue cannot be understated: These were mainly Mexican citizens with little chance of stepping foot in a wrestling ring in America were it not for someone sponsoring them. The cost of these visas to Heyman must have been thousands of dollars at the very least—to anyone who would criticize him for their checks bouncing, one should point out that at least they were not getting deported, thanks to Heyman's visa work. These costs were astronomical for an independent company like ECW, and many in the wrestling business questioned his strategy. The attitude of many is summed up best by Taz, a former ECW Heavyweight Champion.

I had heard of Lucha Libre, but didn't know much about it at the time. Paul was the guy, along with Konnan that brought Rey Mysterio, Super Crazy and Psicosis up. These guys showed up and we were all like, "What the hell is this?!!" Our fans were used to our style of wrestling—hard-core. These Lucha guys were all high-flyers, they wore masks and bright suits. They had a different style, it was pretty wild . . . but no one knew if they were going to go over with the ECW fans.

Whatever crystal ball Heyman used to predict the future did not let him down, as the Lucha Libre stars became a big hit in ECW. The enmascarados were among ECW's most watched wrestlers in America: No one needed to know their characters' backgrounds or needed to hear them talk. They talked with their wrestling moves in an era when there was too much talk and not enough walk in the big two promotions. Heyman showed the WWF and WCW that enmascarados could become popular with the fans because of their unique masks and colorful costumes, not in spite of them. As Taz says, even the wrestlers themselves became enamored of the Luchadores "BIG TIME . . . You couldn't help but admire them: The moves that some of these guys performed were out of this world."

Taz was not alone in his assessments. Much to the two big promotions' surprise, these Lucha Libre wrestlers were causing white American audiences to cheer and fill ECW shows. What WCW conceived of as a one-night-only show, ECW had transformed into a full-time moneymaking gimmick. Americans turned to ECW to watch these Mexican stars. ECW helped take the Luchadores into the mainstream of American wrestling, and the Luchadores helped make ECW into a guerilla-like threat to the WWF and WCW.

Some of the best matches in the history of American professional wrestling—in any era—took place thanks to Paul Heyman's visionary booking, and the explosiveness the Luchadores brought to the ring such as the late great Eddie Guerrero vs. "The Shooter" Dean Malenko in a two-out-of-three-falls series of matches in 1995 for the ECW TV title; Rey Mysterio Jr. vs. Psicosis in a Mexican Death Match at the 1995 November to Remember supercard; and a wonderful match between Rey Mysterio Jr. & Konnan vs. Psicosis & La Parka in late 1995. By the end of 1995, the big two promotions started taking notice.

WCW, led by Eric Bischoff, decided to go on a full offensive against the stuck-in-a-time warp WWF. While the WWF was creating wrestlers with plumber gimmicks, the WCW decided on the whole-sale theft of Heyman's creations. He offered them bucket loads of Ted Turner's money, and Heyman could not afford to compete. In one swoop of the pen, WCW took Guerrero, Malenko, Benoit, Mysterio, Konnan and many other wrestlers from ECW, all at once. Heyman woke up to find his investments of time, money and brainpower gone, in addition to over a third of his roster.

While a sad moment for Heyman and ECW, it was a financial godsend to Luchadores and enmascarados. They had made it to "Where the Big Boys Play," just in time the famous Monday Night Wars between WCW and the WWF. They had gone from being pariahs in the American wrestling business to some of its top stars in WCW. Eddy Guerrero became the WCW U.S. Champion in 1996, not long after he premiered there. And more successes awaited the other Luchadores in that promotion. While the backstage politics was another matter altogether, the public perception was that the Luchadores had achieved the American wrestling dream.

The WWF was slow on its feet to recognize both the hardcore counterculture that ECW was building its success on, and the greater threat that Ted Turner's WCW was providing by appropriating many of ECW's talents. This is not surprising, as the company had been at the top of its game for at least a decade without any viable threat to its supremacy. It is only when some of its biggest home-grown stars—Hulk Hogan, Razor Ramon, and Kevin Nash—left for WCW that it started to worry.

The slow response of the WWF to the Luchador invasion of America could be seen in two failed storylines. First was the way they handled the career of wrestler Al Snow. Snow could wrestle in a multitude of styles, combining high-flying moves with his knowledge of the martial arts. The WWF tried to use its perennial belief in itself to create new stars. Rather than hire any Lucha Libre stars, it decided to try to create its own pseudo-enmascarado out of Al Snow. In October 1995, when real enmascarados Mysterio and Psicosis were having their legendary Mexican Death Matches in ECW, the WWF had Al Snow appear as the masked Japanese wrestler "Avatar." Much was made of Avatar's successes in Mexico, as well. Sound familiar? Yes, it was the machine gimmick back in full force in the WWF. When Avatar failed to fool audiences into thinking that he was a Luchador the WWF repackaged him as the masked "Shinobi the Ninja" in February 1996. In doing this, the WWF revealed its lack of knowledge when it came to creating a true enmascarado.

As demonstrated earlier in this book, a Luchador takes years to develop his gimmick—sometimes decades—a fact the overnight sensation machine that is the WWF could not comprehend. It could not simply transform Al Snow into a Luchador. Every Luchador and enmascarado had his own history, his own tradition, his own origins, and he brought this with him not only in front of the fans in the ring, but backstage as well. Being a Luchador is not something that can be turned on and turned off the way one of the Machines or Doink the Clown or Shinobi could. As Taz observed about the Lucha Libre stars, "It was something [fascinating] to see . . . each one of them had this special link to the past and code they went by. . . . It was pretty cool." If the WWF wanted Luchadores, it would have to swallow its pride and hire some real ones.

In January 1997, facing all-time low ratings against WCW, the WWF did just that and hired wrestlers from the AAA promotion to make a *When Worlds Collide*–like appearance at one of their own pay-per-views, the Royal Rumble. Wrestlers like Cibernético, Latin Lover, Pierroth and even the legendary Mil Máscaras were all participants in the Royal Rumble, making it one of the most high-flying and interesting Rumbles in pay-per-view's history. In addition to Luchadores match, there was also a AAA six-man tag match, pitting Perro Aguayo, Canek & Hector Garza against Fuerza Guerrera, Heavy Metal & Jerry Estrada. That was clearly the match of the night.

But history unfortunately repeated itself: This AAA involvement was for one night only. The WWF did not capitalize upon the success, and decided to let WCW lead the way when it came to Lucha Libre action in America. Critics at the time also pointed out how the WWF now seemed to be reacting to WCW and ECW ideas, rather than generating their own new ones. After all, *When Worlds Collide* occurred in 1995; this was now 1997, and the WWF had just realized that Lucha Libre was a big commodity in American wrestling?

Wherefore the Luchador?

In early 2001, both ECW and WCW ceased to exist. The only major American promotion left was the WWF (soon to become the WWE). Its roster had changed greatly in the four years since the AAA-inspired Royal Rumble: Most of its wrestlers were ECW alumni, with some WCW stars. What is more telling is that still only one Luchador had joined its ranks by January 2001: Eddy Guerrero. And Eddy was pushed as an American-style wrestler: Nothing was made of his Lucha Libre background except an allusion to his "Latino heat."

Not one enmascarado had been hired. The masked wrestlers from ECW and WCW were once again shut out from the American mainstream wrestling market. WWE's new Creative Department, which formed out of the ashes of the departure of intelligent bookers Vince Russo and Ed Ferrera, was concerned with different approaches to wrestling. New Head Writer Chris Kreski's short reign turned in some amazing storylines in late 2000 and early 2001, but Talent Relations gave him no Lucha Libre wrestlers to work with. After Kreski's departure, the WWE Creative turned to stressing comedy—which has arguably led to a decline in its product.

But 2001 saw the hiring of Paul Heyman himself to the WWE. Proving himself to be a Messiah of the Luchadores once again, it was his membership in WWE Creative that led to the hiring of Rey Mysterio Jr. and El Último Dragón—two enmascarados that had made the WCW ring light up whenever they entered it. Without Heyman, these wrestlers could have been forever shut out of the WWE because of their masks. Other Luchadores, like Chavo Guerrero Jr., also joined the WWE's ranks, thanks largely to Heyman's tenure in Creative. He was largely responsible for reinvigorating WWE's cruiserweight division, its Lucha Libre–influenced roster of wrestlers.

Heyman's Lucha Legacy

Heyman, until his unwarranted and ill-advised ouster from WWE Creative in 2003, was busy creating new stars, or reinventing old ones. Most of today's wrestling icons came from the heralded ranks of his ECW. He also brought multiculturalism back to wrestling, tapping into African American culture in the form of gangster rapping (Public Enemy), into Japanese culture (puroresu), and into Latino culture (Lucha Libre). In a world where promoters and their toady writers are largely boors who laugh at fart comedy, Heyman's vision was, and continues to be, a rare breath of fresh air in the professional wrestling world. Heyman's love and respect for other cultures is why we have Lucha Libre stars in America today. When it comes to the surviving Luchadores' current success in America, it is Heyman who should be credited with being their champion. 💀

7

Lucha Is Everywhere

IN NORTH AMERICA there are over one hundred and twenty wrestling promoters and organizations of various sizes. But there is only one major wrestling promoter in the game now—Vince McMahon. He started out in the Northeast with the then WWWF and expanded his empire outward in a case of Manifest Destiny. He engulfed and devoured his competition in a war of contrition until his empire (now legally known as the WWE) controlled the major wrestling business in the country. In contrast, the Lucha Libre wrestling scene in the United States, most of which is in Southern California, is run by independent promoters.

Unlike the established CMLL and AAA promotions in Mexico, the smaller promotions struggle to get the word out about

OPPOSITE: An anxious crowd waits to get inside the arena and cheer their heroes on ABOVE: The next generation of enmascarados

Lucha. Many of these out-of-the-way venues and promoters do nothing more to garner business than hand out flyers or post handbills. There is some advertising in the local Spanish papers, but with the expense of on-air ads in radio and television, much of the public does not know when and where these matches are being held until they hear firsthand. It is a true word-of-mouth movement that needs more voices to sing its praise. Even in the most out-of-the-way venues I have traveled to, I am still amazed to see the amount of fans that show up, often times when the only advertising was a small handbill posted throughout the Mexican neighborhoods.

Whether in Mexico, Southern California, or Chicago (where Lucha events regularly draw fans in the thousands), it seems that the fans instinctively know the rudo and the técnico; they know automatically who to cheer and who to jeer. Even if a certain Luchador is debuting that night, there is a sense of who that wrestler is as he enters the ring. To go to the matches, to watch the Luchadores, to participate as a fan, one has to give himself up to the illusion, to go willingly into the fantasy that is presented to him. Forget whether or not certain things are believable, let alone conceivable.

A perfect example is when I went to a match in South Central one night. It was a trio match, and one team consisted of técnicos: Cassandro, Águila Azteca, and Jaguar de Oro. They came out from behind the small curtain, paraded around the audience to cheers and entered the ring. Then it was the rudos' turn. First out was Doctor Maldad, followed by Monje Maldito and a large man dressed in a Frankenstein mask. The man in the mask wore big, square boots and lumbered around the stage like his living/dead namesake. He didn't pretend to act like the Frankenstein monster; he *was* the Frankenstein monster. To watch the fans react to him was something. The young kids screamed at him while the old ladies hit him when he stalked around the ring; I was watching a cinematic icon come to life before my eyes. No one cared that it was a man in a mask. What they saw was the ultimate rudo, and that is all they wanted.

I believe this was summed up best by Gasparín, *La Voz de la Lucha Libre en California* (The voice of Lucha Libre in California), an exuberant and flamboyant announcer for FCW Lucha promotion, in this simple story. Once, when he was passing out flyers for an upcoming event, a man took one, glanced at it and made a disparaging remark about Lucha being "fake." Gasparín, always the professional, kindly asked the person if he went to the movies. The man said, "Yes, of course I do." Gasparín then asked, "Well, what type of movies do you like to go see?" The man answered, "Action movies." Gasparín replied, "Well, my friend, how can you get more action than going to a Lucha Libre match? There you have action, adventure, drama, comedy, all performed live in front of your eyes. No stunt men, no special effects, all real!"

He is right, everything we go to the movies for is performed on a nightly basis in small venues and large arenas throughout Mexico and Southern California, Southern Texas, and wherever there is a Lucha promotion. Some of the matches I have attended have had thousands of people filling the stands (in the bigger showcase venues) and others have had only a handful of people in the audience. It seems at times there were more wrestlers on the card than in the seats to see them perform, but no matter the size of the crowd, the old adage "the show must go on" rings true when the opening bell sounds.

This brings me to a certain part of wrestling that I am not too comfortable discussing. I worked in professional wrestling, or "the biz," as it's referred to, for a short time. In that time, I met some wonderful people and some real treacherous, lying scumbags—that's life, but I made some very good friends. I was privy to some inside information and riveting stories; of course all of these things

SHAMU

OPPOSITE: Why is Gasparin smiling? You tell me. One of the many perks of being the "Voice of Lucha Libre" in California

were said in total confidence. It is no one's business outside of the promoters, Luchadores, and trainers what goes on behind closed doors in Lucha Libre. The one thing that many people ask me is, "Come on, isn't it all fake?"

I am not going to say whether Lucha Libre, American professional wrestling, or Japanese puroresu is fake or not. These Luchadores, enmascarados and wrestlers are incredible athletes, and it is frustrating to hear naysayers decree that they are not. These men are highly trained and undeniably skillfull. Football players, baseball players, boxers, soccer players—what do they all do? They perform, they excel. We watch in amazement at their skills, talents and dexterity. Wrestlers and Luchadores put on a dramatic story through physicality and emotional mind control—they act, they wrestle, they fight, they make us laugh, they take our breath away. *They* perform, *they* excel.

Is it real or fake? Does it matter? Did you enjoy the show? That is the question you should ask yourself.

Let me sum it up like this: On May 16, 2004, I had the honor to work the Judgment Day pay-per-view in Los Angeles. In that show the late Eddie Guerrero and John "Bradshaw" Layfield (JBL) battled for the WWE Championship. It was considered one of the most brutal and bloody matches in recent wrestling history, both in Lucha Libre and American professional wrestling. JBL defeated Eddie by disqualification (but Guerrero retained the WWE Championship). Both wrestlers were bleeding profusely and the ring looked like the floor of a slaughterhouse. Eddie's face was streaked scarlet (or, as it used to be referred to in the biz, "he was wearing the crimson mask"). Blood shot out of Eddie's head after a brutal chair shot. He was staggering, hurt and battered, but walked out of the ring with his bloody head held up and his championship belt still around his waist. I followed Eddie's trail of blood to the dressing room and then to the hospital, where he was diagnosed with a severe concussion and serious, sustained blood loss. I walked farther down the hall and saw JBL—he was getting his head stapled shut without Novocain. Is that fake? The blood was real, the chairs were real, the pain was real. These men left every ounce of emotion and physical strength in that blood-splattered ring. You tell me, is that fake?

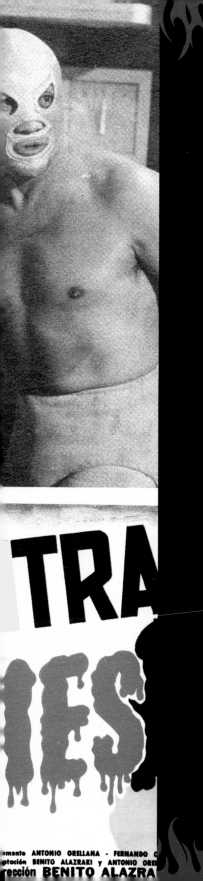

8

Del Anillo a la Pantalla
(From the Ring to the Screen)

LUCHA GOES TO THE MOVIES...

For years, any scholarly book on the subject of Mexican cinema glossed over the Lucha Libre films that Mexico produced. Some film books and journals would give mention to these films with a passing footnote or a small sidebar, but without any real emphasis on what these movies stood for. It is only recently that entire books dedicated to Lucha Libre films hit the bookstores. In the recent past, you had magazines like Cult Movies *or* FilmFax *that would run articles on Lucha films, and then sometime in the nineties* Santo Street *appeared, a fantastic fanzine created by Brian Moran.* Santo Street *was*

OPPOSITE: One of Santo's first encounters with the supernatural: *Santo versus the Zombies,* 1962 **ABOVE:** Thirteen years later, Santo is still fighting the forces of evil: this time it's renegade Nazis

RIGHT: One of the great Lucha films from the imagination of producer/writer Rogelio Agrasánchez

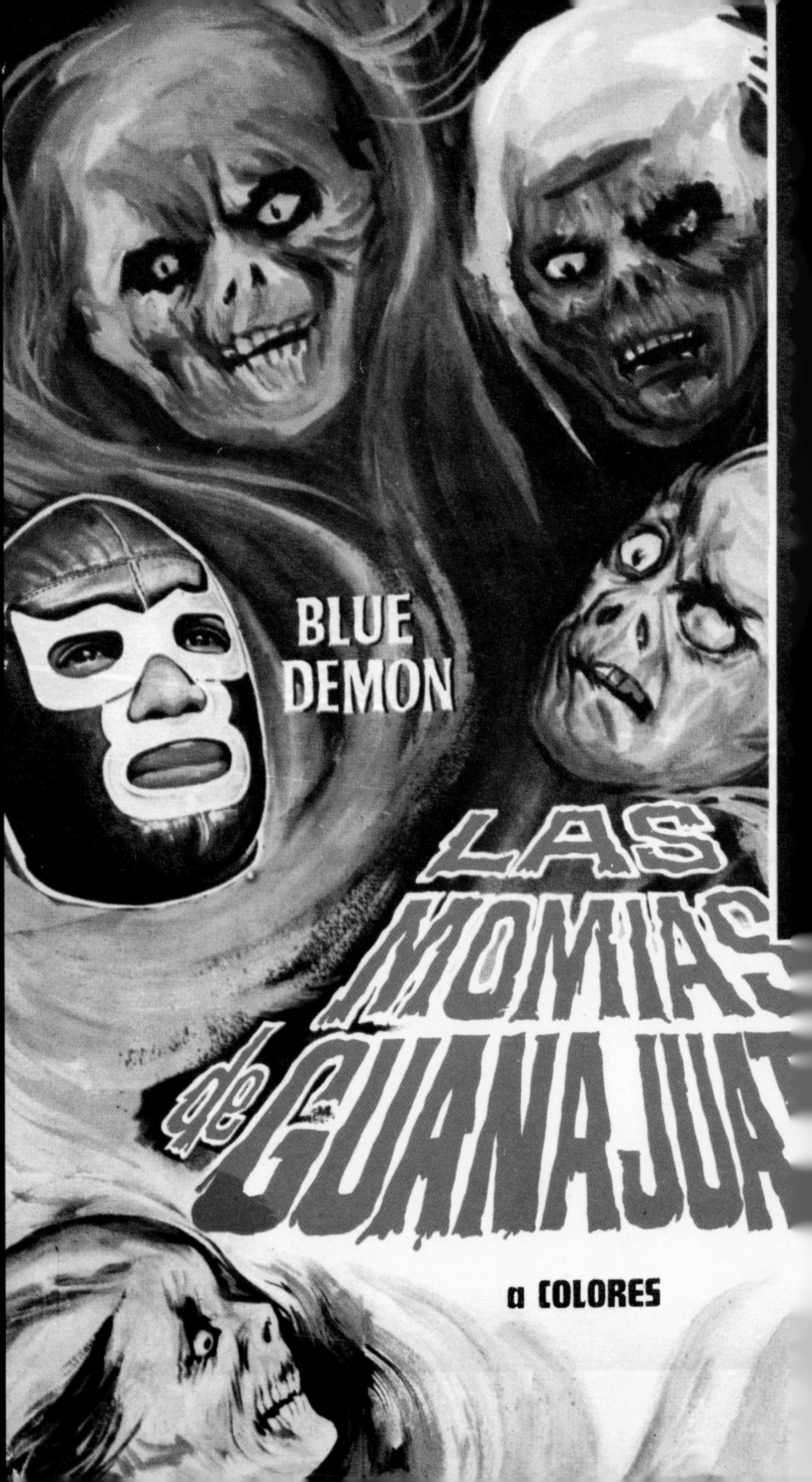
BLUE DEMON
LAS MOMIAS de GUANAJUAT
a COLORES

EL MIL MASCARAS

SENSACIONAL ACTUACION DE:

SANTO

EL ENMASCARADO DE PLATA

CON

ELSA CARDENAS

JUAN GALLARDO - JORGE PINGÜINO

presentación del niño: JULIO CESAR - CARLOS SUAREZ

PATRICIA FERRER - MABEL LUNA - MARTHA ANGELICA

YOLANDA PONCE - DAVID LAMA - CARLOS LEON

argumento original: ROGELIO AGRASANCHEZ-adaptación: RAFAEL GARCIA TRAVESI

cinefotógrafo: ENRIQUE WALLACE - música: GUSTAVO CESAR CARRION

Director: FEDERICO CURIEL

ABOVE: The power of
Satan has nothing on
Blue Demon

OPPOSITE: An
explosive-looking
lobby card from an
explosive film: Neutrón
goes head to head with
the Karate Killers

loaded with information from the filmmakers, the Luchadores, the actresses and everyone else that could be tracked down and interviewed. This is an indispensable treasure trove of information for the Lucha movie fan.

The Lucha films have always been categorized in the fantasy/ horror genre and rightly so; these films have all the elements of the fantastique within them. The uptight film scholars who have routinely dismissed these movies and refrained from giving them even a little recognition have done an enormous disservice to the Mexican film industry, to the Luchadores and Luchadoras who acted in them, to the crews that made them and, most of all, the fans who watched them.

Although Santo is the biggest name in Lucha Libre and in the Lucha movie franchise, he was not the first enmascarado to make movies. The first man to hold that honor was Médico Asesino and his movie was called *El Enmascarado de Plata* (The Man in the Silver Mask). This is where it gets a little confusing. Although the good doctor wore a silver mask very similar to Santo's and despite the fact that Santo became known as El Enmascarado de Plata, he is not in this movie. This film was made in 1952, a full six years before Santo stepped in front of the camera. José G. Cruz, who published the popular Santo comic book, tried to get his star client Santo to be in this picture. When Santo refused, the role went to the popular enmascarado El Médico Asesino.

El Asesino Invisible (The Invisible Killer, aka "The Man in the Gold Mask vs. The Invisible Killer") was another masked superhero who developed in hopes of cashing in on the growing popularity of the Santo franchise. This led to the promising rise of another Lucha film star created just for the screen: El Enmascarado de Oro (Gold Mask), but it seemed in the cinematic world that gold was not as valuable as silver. Gold Mask only made one film. Gold Mask was played by Jorge Rivero, and after his solo foray into leading-man land he became a supporting player in films such as *Los Endemoniados del Ring* (1966), directed by Alfredo B. Crevenna and *Operación 67* (1967), directed by René Cardona and his son René Jr., with Santo in the starring role. Then Rivero went on to star in a couple of wrestling movies called *Lions of the Ring*, directed by Chano Urueta, and eventually went on to an even bigger film career, even starring with John Wayne in *Río Lobo*.

The second enmascarado to step in front of the camera was Huracán Ramírez. It wasn't until 1958—six years after the first Luchador movie—that the man in the silver mask made his film debut. They weren't out to make art, but the movie did succeed financially.

El Santo, in his long film career, made over fifty movies. Add the films of his counterparts and you have well over a hundred and fifty movies. That is a lot of films to ignore, even if you despise the genre, especially since Mexico did not produce a large number of films per

ABOVE: Evil giant spiders from outer space try to conquer the world . . . the only thing in their way is the arachnid-hating Blue Demon

year. But horror films never get the respect due them. So with the bias against the genre, it was disheartening to see the Lucha Libre films, along with their Mexican horror/fantasy counterparts getting very little respect or even attention.

But that has changed. Books like *The Mexican Masked Wrestler and Monster Filmography* by Robert Michael "Bobb" Cotter and Rogelio Agrasánchez's *Mexican Horror Cinema—Posters from Mexican Fantasy Films* finally give these films their due. It was Agrasánchez's father, Rogelio Agrasánchez Sr., who produced some of the better-known Lucha movies in the seventies: *Las Momias de Guanajusto, Vuelven los Campeones Justicieros, Los Campeones Justicieros*, and *Superzan el Invincible*. Those are just a few of the many titles he helped create, and all four of the above mentioned films were directed by the prolific Federico Curiel, who did some great Mexican horror worth tracking down.

LEFT: Mil has a serious disagreement with Los Vampiros de Coyoacán, co-starring with famed Luchador and prolic horror star Nothanael "Franquestein" León

MPIROS
OACAN

las LOBAS DEL RING

Elements in Lucha Libre and the horror genre compliment each other so well; once again, it is good versus evil, mighty hero against the treacherous villain or soulless monster. The enmascarados' careers in the ring and on the screen were virtually interchangeable for the fans. There was no line of demarcation separating the athletic prowess these men showed in the ring and the fantastic powers they possessed while battling monsters in the movies or in the *historietas* (comic books). To the fans, El Santo was the same man who wrestled in the arenas, starred in the films, had adventures in comic books, and walked down the street. He was a tangible superhero, one who lived among his people. No other wrestlers, actors or characters in the entire world had ever had this type of cross-media credence like El Santo. And to some extent Blue Demon and Mil Máscaras had the same, but no one ever rivaled the fans' fervor for the Man in the Silver Mask.

René Cardona Sr. was a filmmaker and something of a visionary of the fantastic, although some have gone as far as calling him the Mexican Trash Maestro. It was Cardona who people credit for starting the Lucha Libre film craze with his 1952 film *El Enmascarado de Plata*. In 1962 Cardona's film *Doctor Doom* took a new turn by casting two female wrestling stars (Luchadoras). In that film, the sister of Gloria Venus (Lorena Velázquez) is kidnapped by a crazed scientist, whose insane experiments have created an apelike monster called Gomar. Gloria and her tag team partner Golden Rubí (Elizabeth Campbell) track down the crazed scientist and battle his evil minions along the way. Several years later, Cardona gave us the splendidly insane movie *Night of the Bloody Apes*, which is more or less a retelling of *Doctor Doom* but in color, very bloody, and with actual footage of a heart operation thrown in for good measure. It also featured a sexy female wrestler dressed in a red kitty devil costume—what's not to love? When Cardona did finally team up with the real El Enmascarado de Plata, they made some of the more popular Santo films from the middle sixties to the early seventies, films such as *Santo vs. El Estrangulador* and its sequel *Espectro del Estrangulador, Operación 67, El Tesoro de Moctezuma, Santo contra Capulina, Santo en el Tesoro de Drácula, Santo contra Los Jinetes del Terror, La Venganza de la Momia,* and *Santo contra los Cazadores de Cabezas.*

ESTUDIOS AMÉRICA
presenta:

FURIAS D

"TURBULENCI
CRIMINAL"
"ZARPAS
TRAICIONER

De la sensacione

LOS

SATADAS

RODOLFO LANDA – ARTURO MARTINE...
MIGUEL MANZANO – ELVIRA QUINTAN...
MARTA E. CERVANTES – SARA GUASH...
EMMA ROLDAN

PELICULAS NACIONALES

CON LOS LUCHADORES
Black Shadow, Sugi Sito,
Dorrel Dixon, Enrique Llanes,
"Murciélago", Frankestein

erie:

TIGRES del RING

La Sombra Vengadora was a masked hero, played by actor Armando Silvestre when not in costume. When La Sombra Vengadora was wearing his mask, the character was played by Fernando Osés. The second movie in the Sombra Vengadora series was *Sombra Vengadora vs. La Mano Negra*. The director of this movie, Rafael Baledón, did some nice monster movies in the '50s and early '60s such as *Hombre y el Monstruo* (Man and the Monster), *Maldición de la Llorona* (Curse of the Crying Woman) and *La Loba*. Fernando Osés was also a screenwriter, as was Jesús "El Murciélago" Velázquez. Enmascarados and Luchadores are a multitalented lot.

And if you have the tendency to appreciate masked women in fetishistic costumes (who in their right minds doesn't?), check out Maura Monti in *Mujer Murciélago* (Batwoman). She wears the sexiest Batman costume knockoff you can imagine. The luscious Ms. Monti also worked in film with the three big names in Lucha, Santo, Blue

Demon and Mil Máscaras in *Santo, el Enmascarado de Plata vs. La Invasión de los Marcianos, Blue Demon, Destructor de Espías,* and *Las Vampiras.*

For the horror film fanatic, get your hands on a copy of *Las Momias de Guanajuato.* Santo, Blue Demon and Mil Máscaras all battle the living dead, but for most of the film Blue Demon and Mil Máscaras fight the rambling zombielike mummies, seemingly losing their side of the struggle. El Santo shows up to save the day, totting handheld flamethrowers, which they use to burn the mummies down to ashes. The next film in this series was titled *Robo de las Momias de Gaunajuato,* but this time around it is Mil Máscaras with Rayo de Jalisco and the Blue Angel fighting once more the forces from beyond the grave (as an added bonus, evil dwarves are sided with the undead against our boys). In the final film of the series, *Castillo de las Momias Guanajuto,* none of the original Luchadores are in it and instead the living dead mummies have a new trio to threaten in Superzan, Tinieblas and Blue Angel.

Some wrestling characters were created especially for the screen because of the huge popularity of Lucha Libre (Mil Máscaras being the most famous of these incarnations). Sometimes these masked actors who had portrayed wrestlers tried their hands in Lucha, but most found it much harder, if not impossible, to go from movies to Lucha. When someone tells you that wrestling is not that hard, ask them when the last time was that they took a chop across the chest or a chair to the head. No matter how tough and strenuous the moviemaking process is—and it is incredibly stressful and hard—it is no match for the world of professional wrestling.

Director Alfredo B. Crevenna's colorful career in Mexican fantastic cinema left a rich legacy for movie fans. Born in Frankfurt, Germany, in 1914, he fled the Nazi regime, moving first to New York, then to Mexico, where he began his film career. Crevenna's work in the Lucha Libre/horror genre includes some of the best and most recognizable titles. Films like *Santo vs. La Magia Negra, Santo y el Águila Real, Santo vs. la Invasion de los Marcianos, La Casa de los Espantos, La Besitas de Terror,* and, one of my personal favorites, *Poder Negro* (Black Power), featuring Mil Máscaras and bodybuilder legend Sergio Oliva, who is so thickly muscled he doesn't look human, let alone mobile. Crevenna helped fill movie theaters with horror movie fans as well as Lucha Libre enthusiasts. But unfortunately that popularity does not translate to easy availability for the seekers trying to find holy grails in the lost annals of dubbed action movies.

Some of these movies made it to American TV through the efforts of the ingenious K. Gordon Murray. He was an American producer and low-end film distributor based out of Florida in the fifties. After working in Hollywood when he was younger, Murray decided to go back home to the Sunshine State and set up show for himself. When Murray realized that importing the Mexican masked wrestler movies into the United States was smart business, he acquired the rights to several Lucha Libre/horror films. He used his own sound recording company, Soundlab, Inc., which was one of the first American companies to re-dub foreign films into English. Murray gave many of the adolescent American Lucha Libre/horror film fans their first taste of those deliciously insane movies from the sixties and seventies in Saturday night late shows throughout the country.

Releasing these films in a television package entitled *The World of Terror* and beginning with the *Nostradamus* series in 1962, Murray showcased some of the most popular titles and series of Mexican horror, including the infamous *Aztec Mummy* series and some incredibly atmospheric vampire films *The Vampire* and *The Vampire's Coffin*. The horror films he imported from Mexico range from some of the finest to some of the weirdest ever to be put on celluloid. Although he tried to be as faithful to the story as possible when rewriting the script from Spanish into English, Murray sometimes dubbed in new dialogue that not only did not coincide with the movie, it actually changed some characters from heroes to villains. Nobody cared; what was important was that he had product—a film he could play for American audiences with exotic foreign locales and beautiful women, monsters and, most of all, masked heroes.

These films began to make their way into the American market, under the mainstream, but at a time when comic books and superheroes were starting to make another surge with the youth of

America. Batman, Spider-Man, Captain America, and other masked do-gooders were once again starting to capture the imagination of teenage boys, and Lucha Libre/horror films seemed like the natural cinematic equivalent. In the re-dubbed American version, Santo is known as Samson. Other Luchadores of note have roles in these movies ranging from supporting parts to cameos, and others appear, such as the stunningly beautiful Luchadora star Lorena Velázquez as Santo's sexy nemesis, Zorina, Queen of the Vampires in *Samson vs. Vampire Women*. In the 1970s K. Gordon Murray ran into a little problem with the IRS, and they confiscated Murray's catalogue of movies. After that, many of these titles seem to have literally vanished. There were smaller video companies putting out some of his titles on the "gray market," but the films that many of us grew up on may just be flickering memories, like the images that played on television so long ago.

It wasn't until several years after Santo started making movies that they appeared in America, and still, most watching these films did not know El Santo was a real-life Luchador in Mexico; many thought he was just a character created for the screen. Santo's career flourished among the fans of these films, and even though the numbers of fans don't rival some of the other heroes of fantastic cinema like Batman or Superman, Santo fans have always been the most loyal and knowledgeable.

Blue Demon's film career is second only to that of his rival/ally El Santo's. Demon's first movie appearances were nothing more than glorified cameos in two productions for producer Alberto López, made in 1961, *Furia de Ring* and *Asesinos de la Lucha Libre*, and did nothing to help jump-start Blue's movie career. It wasn't

ABOVE: It didn't take long before Santo's image was seen on the silver screen, in arenas, and even in comic books

until three years later when Demon left López to work for producer Enrique Vergara, who offered more money and a chance to be a leading enmascarado, did Demon break free of the silvery shadow of El Santo. Blue Demon would have his own starring role with his own colorful moniker in the title. His first lead in a motion picture was called *Blue Demon el Demon Azul,* directed by Chano Urueta. Demon's movie career seemed to be heading in the right direction, but in 1965, during a match, Blue Demon suffered what could have been a life-ending injury. Kicked in the head by an opponent, Demon crashed to the cement floor headfirst. Being a true professional and one tough, proud *hombre,* Demon got up from that devastating tumble and did not receive medical ringside assistance from anyone. Later on in his hotel, he collapsed and fell down a flight of stairs, and was immediately rushed to the hospital and into surgery. He had a fractured skull and severe brain edema. For the rest of 1965 Blue Demon was on the mend, and his professional wrestling and movie careers had to be put on hiatus until the brave enmascarado was well enough to return. But that left his producer in a bind. Luis Vergara was a man who saw opportunity everywhere and he saw it in a twenty-six-year-old Olympic judo hopeful named Aaron Rodríguez, who decided to forgo amateur judo for professional wrestling. Mr. Rodríguez would acquire the colorful name of Mil Máscaras and become one of Lucha's biggest wrestling and movie stars in the years to come.

Mil Máscaras, the Man of a Thousand Masks, came to life on the big screen in 1966. Mil Máscaras's persona was designed specifically for the movies, a prefabricated film character. When his popularity in cinema grew, the Lucha Libre fans clamored to see their new screen hero in the flesh, and Mil made his debut in the ring. Athletically trained and physically gifted, Mil became a fan favorite overnight. He starred in almost twenty movies in twenty-five years.

The Lucha Libre/masked wrestling movie era slowly died out in the '70s, and by the early '80s only a handful of movies were made. Today, one or two films trickle out every so often starring the Son of Santo and other wrestlers. But the Golden Age of the enmascarado ruling the silver screen is gone. But not all is lost; with the emergence of video and now DVDs, many of these titles are available and worth searching out.

Lucha fans, once bitten by the movie bug, became ravenous; their appetite is uncontrollable when it comes to tracking down these "genre" or "cult" films. And the influence of these films on other international filmmakers is obvious. Mario Bava's delicious comic book film *Danger: Diabolik* (although based on an existing character) was inspired by the Santo films. This wasn't the only Italian try at the enmascarado genre; the 1968 outing *Goldface il Fantastico Superman* (Goldface, the Fantastic Superman) was directed by Bitto Albertini. Goldface, played by Robert Anthony (real name Espártaco Santoni), is clearly inspired by Santo—Gold Mask is by day a crime fighter and by night a masked wrestler fighting evildoers in Caracas. Another Italian enmascarado to hit the screen was Superargo, and once again the job requirements meant fighting crime from nine to five and wrestling opponents once the sun went down.

Even though the Santo movie craze didn't penetrate the United States at this time, the Mexican films did find it easier to enter the European marketplace. Lucha Libre's influence on fantastic cinema cannot be overlooked or under praised. These films set the standard (sometimes that standard was abysmally low for quality and storytelling capabilities) but nonetheless the overall visual strength and supercharged heroes caught on throughout the world well enough that every country wanted to give a crack at creating an enmascarado-like hero. The strength, style and influence of Lucha Libre was just taking hold.

ABOVE: The art of the lobby card is unique: girls, guns, and action; eye-catching and enchanting for an impressionable youngster

GOSPEL TRUTHS OF LUCHA MOVIES

by Keith J. Rainville

In a film genre that, by its very existence, seemingly defies all logic and common sense, there are some steadfast rules. Consider these among the Laws of Lucha Cinema Nature:

First, no matter what threat to humanity looms or how heated a conflict is with a potentially world-crippling super-villain, nothing ever cancels that night's wrestling match!

Remember, the Luchador is just that—a wrestler. Sure, he'll save the world, but he's just moonlighting as a superhero. Enmascarados would drop their wire cutters and leave a ticking time bomb if it was getting close to bell-time. Monsters are left to prowl, madmen roam the streets and kidnap-victims suffer in bondage while these men-of-action stop everything on a dime, don their capes and pay the rent. It would be very unpleasant to be a damsel in distress, tied to the train tracks, if across town your hero was more concerned with lacing his boots. Fear the death ray. Fear the killer ape. Fear the mad scientist. But fear the scorned wrestling promoter more!

BELOW: Cavernario Galindo, Blue Demon, Black Shadow, Gory Guerrero, and Bobby Bonales: good luck trying to find another group as tough as this one

There's always time for a cocktail and a musical number.

If there's time to forget the atomic bomb about to go off somewhere in Mexico City to engage in a two-out-of-three-falls tag team bout, then there's certainly time to take a date to a cabaret and catch a nice jazzy lounge number or two. Record labels and concert promoters co-opted blocks of time in these movies, and damn it, their acts were going to be seen, no matter what conflict was going on around them.

Anyone in a wrestling audience wearing sunglasses is up to no good.

True without variance, and a staple of the genre. Amid a heated crowd of animated wrestling enthusiasts, one sits sternly, unmoving, calmly watching from behind a pair of knockoff Ray-Bans. Watch out for this guy! He's got a killer robot in his basement, or is the hired hit man for a hooded maniac.

Midget henchmen are good.

Atomic-powered midget henchmen are better. The little people do not fare well in the world of the enmascarado superhero, and there were no anti-dwarf-tossing laws in Mexico during the golden age of Lucha films!

A color-themed masked wrestler cannot color-coordinate his wardrobe to save his life.

The beloved Blue Demon is the trade's finest example of this categorical fashion ineptitude. Your name is "Blue Demon." You wear a blue wrestling mask all day every day. You'd think you'd have a coordinated blue wardrobe, right? No way. Blue would routinely appear in something like brown slacks, a rusty orange sport coat and olive-green shirt with yellow collar and cuffs, accented with a maroon and white polka-dotted tie, and white vinyl loafers.

The daughters of any man of science are always smoking hot!

This is an axiom of sci-fi and horror cinema worldwide, but in Mexico, it's a set-in-stone law. Any professor, criminologist or research scientist caught up in some bizarre plot, be he a plump balding brainiac or a bespectacled bookworm, has

ARIADNE WELTER

"TONGOLELE" - ERIC DEL CASTILLO

EDA LORNA en

LAS MUJER

con

JENARO

MARIA

JORGE MONC

la niña ELEN

ARS UNA
PUBLICIDAD

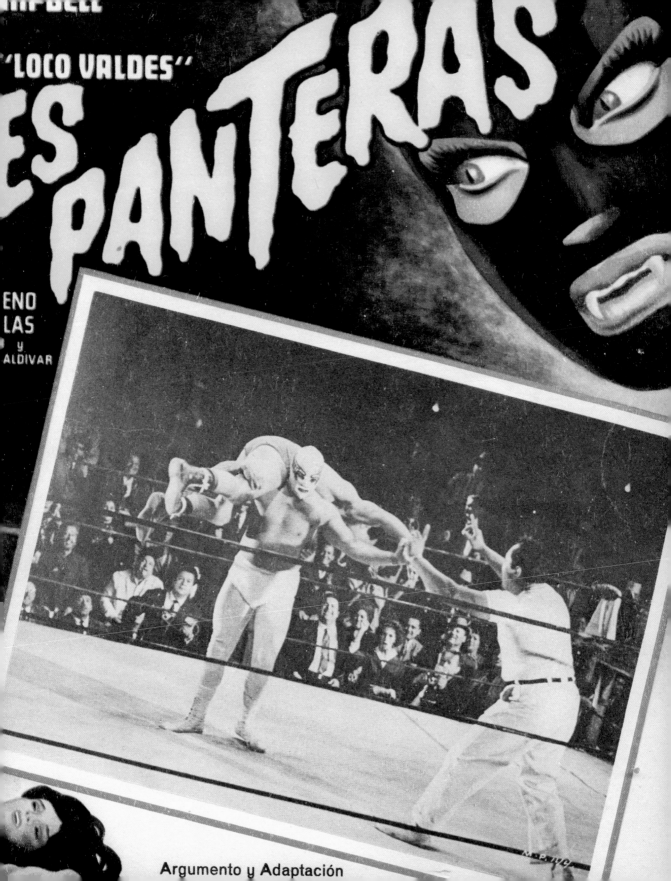

ABOVE: Santo and Blue Demon fight underwater Nazis in the lost world of Atlantis . . . and yes, that is a believable story line

a knockout siren for a daughter. And you never see the mom who produced this physical marvel with this dork, either.

If you're going to wear a cape, drive a convertible!

Santo was typically depicted driving a stylish two-seater, white or silver, often a Jaguar, Mercedes, or Mexican knockoff on an MG spider. This allowed him an easy exit to jump into action, and that dashing sequined cape to flow over the back of the trunk in a most majestic fashion. As the genre waned and the budgets for the pictures got smaller, the cool sports cars were replaced by a motley variety of less-than-impressive compromises—dune buggies, beater Mustangs with broken taillights, some type of south-of-the-border equivalent to a Dodge Dart, and even wood-panel station wagons—basically anything the producer's brother would loan him from his used car lot in Juárez.

Lucha Talent = Easy Street for Film Producers

Imagine you're a film producer with a limited budget, but big audience potential. It's an exploitation situation, and proven things always put bottoms in seats—monsters, hot chicks, gore, car chases, etc. Hiring a masked wrestler as your picture's principal doesn't seem like the first thing that would occur to most, but when you look at what an established enmascarado superstar can bring to your production, it makes Mexi-Lucha common sense:

Wrestlers do their own fights. The scripts for these films are riddled with blank spots, annotated with the accepted vernacular "Insert wrestling fight here." No stunt doubles, no fight coaches or martial arts wire crews needed. Show the wrestler what patch of grass he can use, and he starts slapping dudes around and monkey-flipping your flick to profitability!

The full head mask has its advantages. In cases where you do need a stunt double, and it wasn't that frequent, the full head covering makes doubling quite easy. Thus, you had enmascarados as adept at horseback tricks as they were headlocks, or diving off a fifty-foot cliff like it was a five-foot ring post. Another huge advantage of the hood was that it obscured the mouth. These films were primarily shot silent, with all the voices dubbed in later in post. Wrestlers' voices were mostly replaced with those of bold, deep-voiced actors, and the covered mouths made this otherwise difficult sync a snap.

Wrestlers bring their own costumes. No self-respecting ring star would trust some motley film studio's costume department for his movie wear. Wrestlers were already well equipped with their signature masks and tights, plus a dazzling array of shiny capes or jewel-encrusted toreador jackets to accent the whole look. It also goes without saying that a man in a full head mask doesn't need hair or makeup. . . .

Wrestlers have weird and cool pals to be in your movie, too. Hire Santo, and you get Santo's manager along for the ride to play a mad scientist or comedy sidekick. Hire Blue Demon and you get his tag team partner Black Shadow as a heavy for the bad guys. Need some thugs or bank robbers the next day? The wrestler makes a few calls, and boom, you've got a battle royale's worth of musclemen on set in a matter of minutes. Watch a flick like the highly recommended *Santo y Blue Demon contra los Monstruos*, and you'll see these amazing zombie henchmen that look to be in full "undead" latex appliances. What they really are are fellow wrestlers like Cavernario (Caveman) Galindo, whose ringscarred face was so pocked and striated, simple green face paint did the trick!

Every time a wrestler enters a ring, he's doing P.R. for your studio. Santo packed arenas every week, had people glued to their TVs and sold a million comic books a week. You put him on the silver screen and you hardly needed an ad budget. The bigger a program the wrestler was involved in ring-wise, the better the movies would perform around him.

Wrestlers can sell any situation! And this, above all, is why these guys really worked as action heroes. Take a man willing to make a living by wearing a shiny head mask and matching tights, performing ritualized combat half-naked in front of thousands of leering fans. This is not a man who's going to balk at the notion of getting in a fistfight with a wolf man. He's not going to be above acting terrified when attacked by the world's worst-built giant rubber octopus. He can battle goofy costumed aliens and trash a plywood lab like he was a Viking berserker on a pillaging rampage, and do it with conviction! There's an innate honesty to the actions these men took on film, and it carries. When Santo burst into a burning orphanage to save those poor kids, everyone in the audience could believe he was in peril, could believe he was overcoming that peril with pure heart and courage. They could believe it, because Santo himself believed it. That ability to sell a situation was learned in the squared circle.

So You Want to Buy a Lucha Film?

Let's be frank here. This is a, shall we say, quality-challenged genre. Sure, there's some real amazingness out there, and just about any Lucha film will have a decent match or one standout scene. But to get the most for your buck, or for those about to take the plunge and buy your first Flex-Mex flick, keep the following in mind:

Don't speak Spanish? No subtitles? No worries! A select few of these films made it to DVD with English subs, but more and more are coming out for the Latino markets. Don't let this be

a deal-breaker! These are very primary films with simple good vs. evil messages, and genre elements familiar to any horror, sci-fi or comic book fan. You'll be able to follow the action no problem, and truthfully, sometimes not knowing how bad the dialogue is can be a blessing.

Black and White = Better. True in many ways. The films from the early days of the genre had better budgets, fresher approaches, and younger stars who were in better fighting shape and more active on screen. They were inspired by the Universal Monsters films, and reflected a moodier, more classic horror feel, peppered with some fine space-age sci-fi spice. These movies watch like Golden Age comic books read, and there's some legit good genre filmmaking here by any standard.

Color = Schlock, but cheese can be good, too. In different ways, the color films have their own appeal. The stars are older, and spend less time bare-chested, more time in bad leisure suits. The budgets were less, and color film exposes the cheapness of the sets and props more than atmospheric black-and-white did. BUT, these films certainly have their "psychotronic" value, often so bad they're good. The women get less attractive than their bee-hived statuesque predecessors, but the musical numbers get weirder and weirder.

Wrestling fans, early films are for you. Mexico does not have a good history of archiving television, and there is precious little ring footage from the Golden Age of Lucha Libre. Fortunately, these films were usually padded with at least one or two wrestling matches. Some were staged for the film crews, but others were shot vérité in steamy arenas packed with throngs of rabid fans. The black-and-white films in particular are a treasure trove of Lucha history, with Santo, Blue Demon, and other ring legends at their prime.

You can't go wrong with team movies. If you couldn't get Santo, you could still pack a theater by teaming up a bunch of not-quite-so-legendary masked men as a colorful fighting unit. Enmascarados in packs of three to six formed teams like Mexican Super Friends or Justice Leagues. These were often anchored by a big star like Blue Demon or Mil Máscaras, filled out with up-and-comers like sci-fi hero Superzan or the towering Tinieblas, and even some never-before-(and never again)-

seen new gimmicks. Team movies mean more wrestlers, more villains and more fights!

Genre completists take note! Are you a Frankenstein freak? Better have *Santo y Blue Demon contra los Monstruos* in your collection. "Franquestein" has a fashionable goatee, and even drives a getaway car! Gore hounds will love the brutality of flicks like *Night of the Bloody Apes* or *Santo contra la Hija de Frankenstein*. Zombie fanatics, understand that the word *momia* does not always refer to a bandaged-wrapped Egyptian automaton. Rather, Mexico has its own breed of zombie, in spired by the alkalai soil-preserved corpses on display in the city of Guanajuato. These "mummies" come to life all the time, behaving just like a ragged and rotting Romero reject, until a colorful masked wrestler buzz-kills their good times with a flamethrower. Horror fans should pay particular attention to the Lucha film genre, as it has its own version of everything from Dracula to the Creature from the Black Lagoon to the Phantom of the Opera.

The power of cinema is a tremendous force to be reckoned with. For a few hours we are at repose. The worries of the world do not matter once the lights go down and the first images flicker on the screen. It is the same feeling of exhilaration one feels when the arena lights dim and the Luchador marches into the ring; time stands still. Nowhere do those feelings of complete apprehension, contentment, excitement and suspense mingle together in the way that they do in Lucha Libre wrestling and cinema. The merger of these two art forms was inevitable, and it helped transcend both parts into a whole. For over three decades one could not think of Lucha Libre without thinking of the films that accompanied them and vice versa. In fact, most of the world knew Santo from the big screen rather than the wrestling ring. It is easier to remember Santo today as a movie star than by the matches he wrestled, the fabled battles that made him a star. They do not exist except in the memories of those lucky enough to have watched him perform. 💀

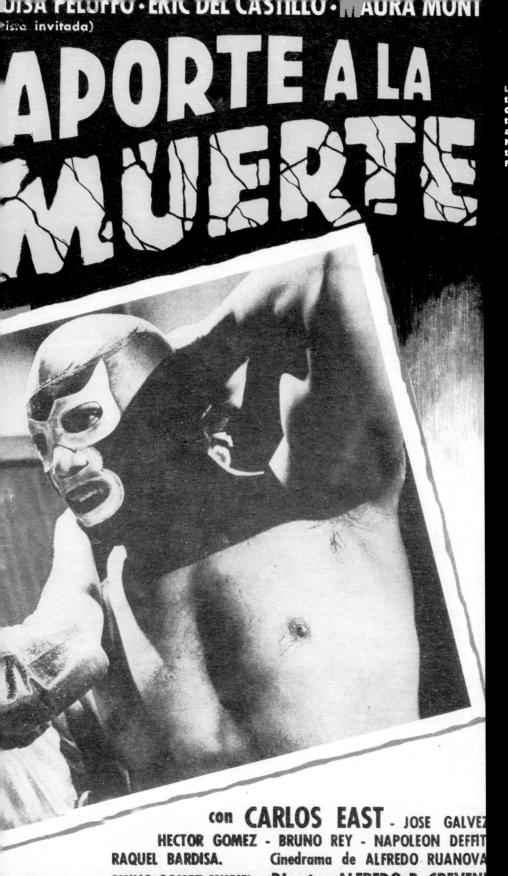

LUISA PELUFFO · ERIC DEL CASTILLO · MAURA MONTI
(ista invitada)

APORTE A LA MUERTE

con **CARLOS EAST** · JOSE GALVEZ
HECTOR GOMEZ · BRUNO REY · NAPOLEON DEFFIT
RAQUEL BARDISA. Cinedrama de ALFREDO RUANOVA
EMILIO GOMEZ MURIEL · Director ALFREDO B. CREVEN

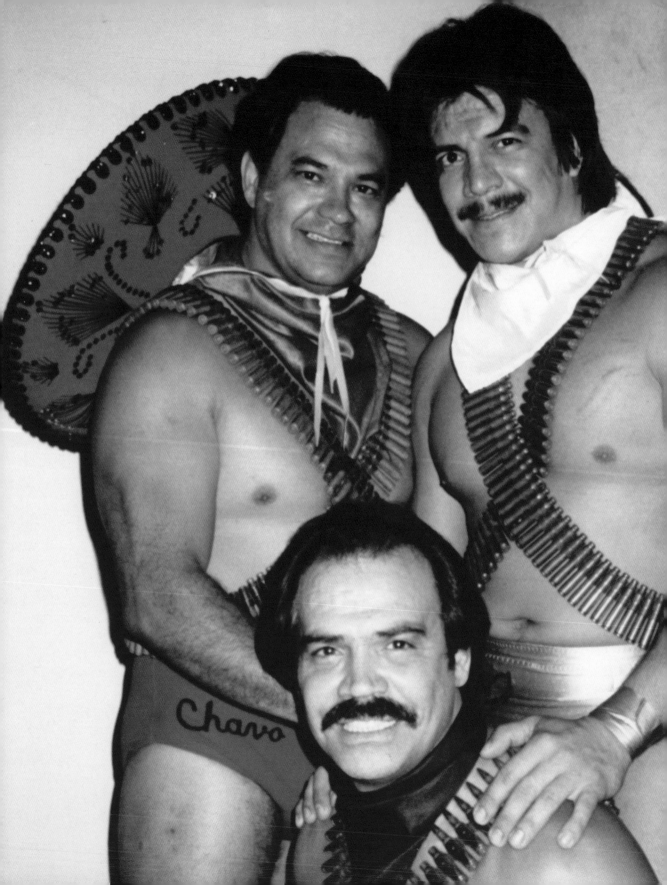

9

La Edad Dorada

La Edad Dorada de Lucha Libre: Las Leyendas, Las Peleas, Los Fósforos Del Resentimiento
(The Golden Age of Lucha Libre: The Legends, the Feuds, the Grudge Matches)

Gory Guerrero

Gory Guerrero was without a doubt one of the most beloved and respected Luchadores in the history of all professional wrestling. He was born Salvador "Gory" Guerrero Quesada in Ray, Arizona, on January 11, 1921. He moved with his family to Guadalajara, Mexico, when he was thirteen. Because of his bilingual skills, Gory was able to help support his family as an interpreter in a pottery shop. While Gory was still a boy his mother passed away, and so the young Guer-

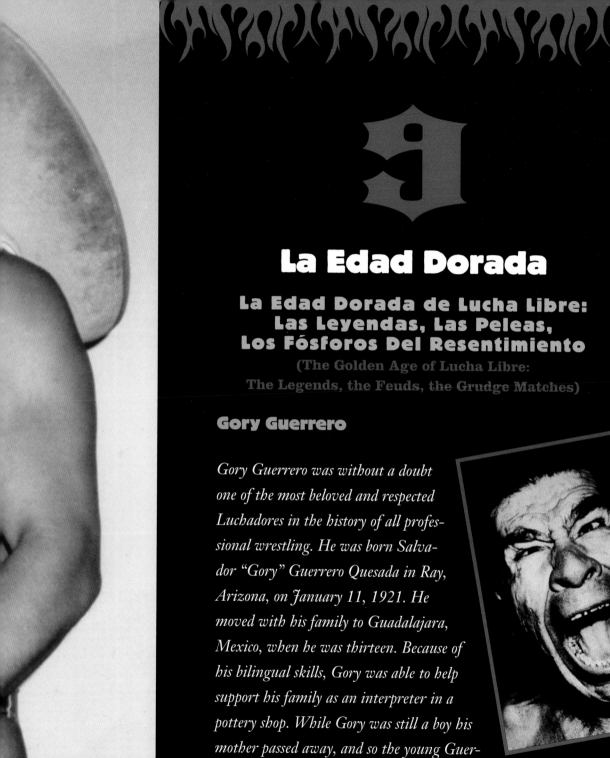

OPPOSITE: Three members of Lucha's most respected family: Chavo, Héctor, and Mando, sons of the great Gory Guerrero ABOVE: A face only a mother could love (maybe): Cavernario Galindo shows why he caused many opponents to have nightmares

rero went on to find ways to help his family. He worked the gambit from paperboy to bellboy to baker's assistant.

Gory was a naturally gifted athlete, and his first inclination was to become a boxer. He trained at Box y Lucha Club for free to get his first taste of life inside the ring. However, after watching the Luchadores working out, the wrestling bug bit Gory, and whatever dreams he had of putting on the gloves evaporated. Gory's first trainers were the soon-to-be legendary Diablo Velazco and El Indio Mejía. Lucha Libre was still a growing sport back then so even the trainers had a lot to learn, as Gory would say later on. Everyone gained experience the only way they could—they wrestled and wrestled hard. Gory had his debut match at the tender age of sixteen in front of his new home crowd of Guadalajara in the small Arena Nilo on September 14, 1937. A whopping 15 *centavos* was his purse for defeating Raf "El Rojo," but it wasn't the money that compelled him to return for more. He was hooked. Gory loved to train and his physique showed the hours he spent in the gym. He quickly became a crowd favorite as he plied his trade in small venues and out-of-the-way arenas working for small promoters.

To establish a Luchador with the fans, a smart promoter will have his top técnico feud with his top rudo—there is nothing like a good old-fashioned blood rivalry to put people in the seats. Throughout Gory's long career he would have some brutal battles with some of the top Luchadores in the business. He started his run of feuds against men like Firpito Bustos, Chimal Galón and Zandokan in the local arenas as his reputation started to grow.

It was during this period that Gilberto Martínez Larrea saw the young Gory and was astounded by his potential. Larrea became something of a mentor to Gory and taught him how to "shoot" in a match if necessary. The "shoot" techniques are indispensable; they allow a wrestler to handle himself if things in a match get too out of control, and if his opponent needs to be taken out quickly. Another man who impacted Gory's career was wrestler Raúl Romero. He taught him amateur wrestling techniques that helped round out his repertoire of in-ring skill.

Gory's technical proficiency was growing at a rapid pace at a young

OPPOSITE: **Gory Guerrero and his family with his championship belt: all his sons would join the family business—Chavo, Héctor, Mando, the late Eddie, and even grandson Chavo Jr.**

age. It wasn't long before the powerhouse of Lucha Libre took notice of Gory. He was called up to the big leagues, and on January 3, 1943, he made his debut match working EMLL. His growth and expertise garnered him the Rookie of the Year award. A championship was not too far away from Gory's reach, and on April 20, 1945, he defeated the celebrated American expatriate Jack O'Brien to win the National Welterweight title. But he was forced to abdicate his new crown after a week for failure to make weight requirements. Gory would become ravenous to attain another championship. So after wrestling harder than before, he had his second shot at the gold. He defeated tough Bobby Bonales on September 25, 1945, to win the National Middleweight title. Gory held on to that title against all comers but he lost the belt to none other than El Santo—a man who would be intertwined with Gory's life and career for the next several decades.

The feud that would really establish Gory as an all-out Luchador superstar was the rivalry he had with Cavernario Galindo; these battles started in the late 1940s and continued on into the early 1950s. These weren't so much Lucha matches as they were all-out blood baths. The intensity and brutality that both of these men brought to the ring is now legendary, and it was their blood-soaked encounters that fueled the Golden Age of Mexican Lucha Libre. Later Gory teamed up with the man who took his middleweight title, El Santo. The two became the famous La Pareja Atómica (The Atomic Pair). Now these two extraordinary athletes battled Cavernario Galindo and his new partner, the phenomenal Black Shadow. These four men gave the fans some of the greatest matches in the sport's history.

The feuds between La Pareja Atómica and Cavernario Galindo and Black Shadow were some of the best "gates" in the business—tickets sold out quickly. Fans who were not lucky enough to get tickets would stand outside the arenas and listen to the crowds inside. Gory also wrestled as a singles competitor and he fought and defeated his idol Carlos "Tarzán" López to win the NWA World Middleweight title. Gory walked away with the moniker of *consagrado*—he had achieved superstar status. Gory went on to have classic rivalries against some of the toughest names in the business.

A true pioneer in Lucha, Gory even has signature moves named after him; *la De a Caballo* (the Camel Clutch) and the Gory Special (a hanging backbreaker submission hold with devastating results) were two destructive legendary finishing moves. The battles of the Lucha ring began to take their toll on Gory's body (they do with all Luchadores). He started to lighten up his hectic wrestling schedule, choosing to showcase in only a handful of cities in America and Mexico. As Gory neared the end of his in-ring career, he slowly started to change his focus and became a trainer, always teaching to most important aspect of Lucha—the respect for the business at all times. Gory was also a booker, running shows in El Paso and in Juárez.

The Lucha Libre bloodline in the Guerrero family is one of the strongest in the world. His sons Chavo, Mando, Hector, and Eddie and grandson Chavo Jr. have all entered the Lucha ranks to great success. They all carried on the tradition of hard work, skill, toughness and integrity that was passed down from their father and grandfather. Gory left this world April 18, 1990. He was surrounded by his family. His legacy still lives on, and his importance to Lucha Libre can never be understated.

Ray Mendoza and Los Villanos

Ray Mendoza was born José Díaz Velázquez on July 6, 1929, in Mexico City. Growing up poor and underprivileged led young Ray to the conclusion that he better learn to fend for himself the right way or face the reality of getting beaten up by the older boys. He joined a gym called Gimnasio Gloria to learn how to box. He only wanted to learn the basics to defend himself properly, but he was spotted by trainer Juan "El Charrito" Espinoza, who had him entering the pro ranks shortly after.

Life was hard at this time for Ray. Not only was he training to be a professional prizefighter, but he was up all night working at his job in a bakery and supporting his wife, Lupita Mendoza, whom he had married at age fifteen. Ray boxed under the name Joe Díaz, but his boxing career was cut short after having a fall-out with Espinoza over a trivial matter. The angered trainer then had some Luchadores spar with the inexperienced youngster to teach him a lesson. Ray may have been able to handle himself standing up but the mat is a whole other world. Not yet versed in the art of Lucha Libre, Ray suffered a bad back injury and his boxing career was over. It is sad that his trainer would put the young Ray in such a precarious situation, but the boxing world's loss would be the Lucha world's gain.

Ray stayed at the gym and continued training to strengthen his body and rehabilitate himself. Efrén "Ray" Carrasco, the owner of the gym, noticed him after his physique started to fill out due to the strenuous weightlifting regime he was undergoing. Carrasco approached Ray with the idea of becoming a Luchador. The idea intrigued Ray; he never forgot the embarrassing and painful beating he took from the Luchadores who hurt his back. To learn to fight in the Lucha style was undoubtedly appealing. From Carrasco he learned amateur wrestling, submission fighting and the basic tenants of mat work. After Ray showed a natural aptitude for grappling, he was introduced into the Lucha Libre style of wrestling. His Lucha trainers were Rogelio de la Paz, Genaro Contreras, Raúl Rojas, and Daniel García, who was not quite yet the star he would become under the name Huracán Ramírez.

Ray's official debut was in 1953 in Monterrey, where he wrestled under the nom de guerre "El Pelón" (Baldy) Chato Díaz. Not happy with that moniker, he went through several name changes that included El Rayo Rojo, "Indio" Mendoza, El Hombre del Rayo Rojo, and he even had a try at being an enmascarado while wrestling under the name Gargantúa. He finally decided on Ray Mendoza after his trainer Ray Carrasco, and he took his beloved wife's maiden name Mendoza in honor of his love for her. Ray wrestled as a rudo, a wrestler the crowds loved to hate. He was tough, had taken his training seriously and was being looked at by higher ups in the Lucha Libre world.

Ray was called up to EMLL by Salvador Lutteroth himself and put in a Battle Royal against the top five Luchadores in the world: Black Shadow, Blue Demon, Cavernario Galindo, Gory Guerrero, and El Santo. This "rub" by the top names in the business only helped Ray to the top. He teamed with two future legends in their own right, René Guajardo and Karloff Lagarde; the formation of this terrific trio of

rudos brought years of notoriety and prosperity for Ray. It wasn't long before he turned the tables on his stablemates Guajardo and Lagarde and became a técnico and a fan favorite. Guajardo and Ray had some classic hair vs. hair matches and the former friends (turned bitter rivals) were great for the box-office sales. Things looked great for Ray's future: He had some classic feuds with Guajardo that would become part of his lore, he had fought some controversial matches with a young upstart rudo enmascarado named El Solitario, and the crowds loved the converted técnico Ray Mendoza.

But there was trouble brewing within the ranks of EMLL when Salvador Lutteroth Sr., the man responsible for the phenomenal growth of Lucha Libre throughout Mexico, stepped down as the head of the organization he started forty years earlier, leaving a power vacuum. At the same time, three of Ray's sons had joined the ranks of Lucha as a masked trio of rudos called Los Villanos. Although they worked for the same company their father worked for, now run by Lutteroth's sons, they were not highly regarded. Ray became increasingly frustrated that his sons would not get the support they needed to succeed. Ray decided to leave the company that had put him on the map. Along with his rivals, Karloff Lagarde and René Guajardo, and his trio of rudo sons, Los Villanos. Ray started a new Lucha Libre organization.

The newly formed La Alianza de la Lucha Libre Internacional, S. C. was born. The company would become known internationally as UWA (Universal Wrestling Association). UWA had top-name Luchadores associated with it and pulled in other wrestlers who were not happy with EMLL. This business rivalry between former employer and former employees would heat up, and it would be the fans who would benefit most from the schism. The more the heated rivalry, the more the warring promotions tried to outdo each other with talent and matches. Ray continued to wrestle into the seventies, but as he got on in years he stopped wrestling and mainly concentrated on his sons and training younger wrestlers; he even captured the post of lead commissioner of the Comisión de Box y Lucha del Distrito Federal. Eventually UWA would fold after giving CMLL (formerly EMLL) a run for their money, showing the world that CMLL was not the powerhouse they had been years before.

Ray Mendoza was a highly respected man in the world of Lucha and his death in April 2003 caused much shock and sorrow. His death did not stop his influence on the sport he loved; his sons followed in their famous father's footsteps. Five of his offspring have become known collectively as Los Villanos, a villainous brood of enmascarados that have grown into one of the major forces in Lucha history. The fighting family first consisted of the three eldest sons, Villano I (Villano Primero): José de Jesús Díaz Mendoza, Villano II (Villano Segundo): José Alfredo Díaz Mendoza, Villano III (Villano Tercero): Arturo Díaz Mendoza, each one trained by his father, and the famed Bobby Bonales and Felipe Ham Lee had a hand in teaching the tricks of the trade to the terrible trio. After Villanos I and II passed away, the two youngest sons picked up the mantle and became Villanos IV and V, and along with Villano III, they are still one of the most respected and feared forces in the sport.

Tarzán López

Lucha Libre legend Tarzán López came into this world as Carlos López Tovar on August 28, 1912, in Jerez, Zacatecas. López's first athletic endeavors were in the "sweet science"—he wanted to be a professional fighter. But boxing lost another potential superstar to the Lucha bug.

López made his pro debut as Carlos López on April 12, 1934. He beat Enrique Gonzalez at Arena Peralvillo-Cozumel in Mexico City, and from then on his career was on a trajectory upward, especially when he hooked up with legendary trainer Diablo Velazco. With Velazco in his corner López had his first classic feud with a muscular and rugged Luchador named Salvador Flores, whose nickname was "Hercules del Ring." But Lopez was something of a physical specimen himself; his athletic build led the fans to call him "Tarzán" and it fit him. For not only was he an impressive-looking guy, he could fight. He was a feared "submission" fighter or "shooter." Nobody wanted to get on Tarzán's bad side in a brawl. Tarzán defeated Mario Nuñez and won his first title, the National Welterweight Championship on March 11, 1936. The legend was born.

Throughout the early forties Tarzán entertained the crowds, and won several more titles and many awards as Luchador of the year in 1940, '44 and '48. He was without a doubt the biggest attraction in Lucha for the first part of that decade and that was proven when he christened the EMLL's new Lucha venue, La Arena Coliseo. Tarzán won that night, though his opponent—none other than El Santo—put him through a brutal battle. The pair would battle again in the years to come and put on some incredible displays of athleticism and physicality. Santo himself said that the toughest man he ever faced and the most skillful Luchador he ever battled was Tarzán. Santo had nothing but praise for López, and looked up to the man who engaged him in so many battles and made him a better wrestler.

In 1946 Lopez fought Gory Guerrero and lost, but the match further galvanized both men's already stellar reputations. Tarzán wrestled for years, always drawing huge crowds. He left EMLL when the notoriously cheap company would not agree to loan Tarzán money he desperately needed for a friend—not the way to treat a man who helped establish your company and put Lucha Libre on the map. It was easier getting blood from a stone than money from the Lutteroths, and the funds they had in their coffers were earned by the blood and sweat of the very men they refused to share it with. So Tarzán retired from the ring and lived a very comfortable retirement from the investments he made off his ring earnings.

The Black Shadow

His name sounds like something out of an old crime fiction pulp paperback, but there was nothing fictitious about the fierce Black Shadow. Born Alejandro Cruz Ortiz on May 3, 1921, in the city of León, Guanajuato, Cruz's first ambitious were musical. He would eventually choose to express his artistry in the wrestling ring instead. Cruz had always been a big fan of Lucha Libre and some of the

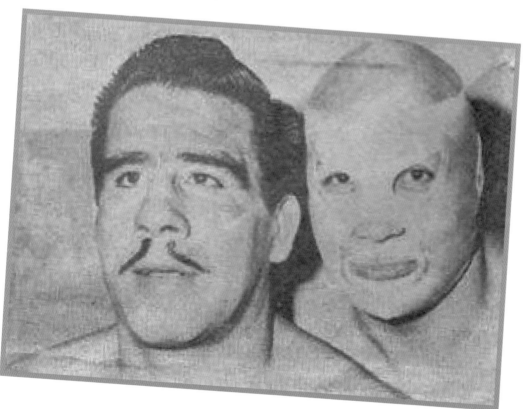

EL MUNDO DEL RING

box y lucha

No. 740

$1.00

CUANDO
SIENTA
MIEDO ME
Retiraré
CASSIUS

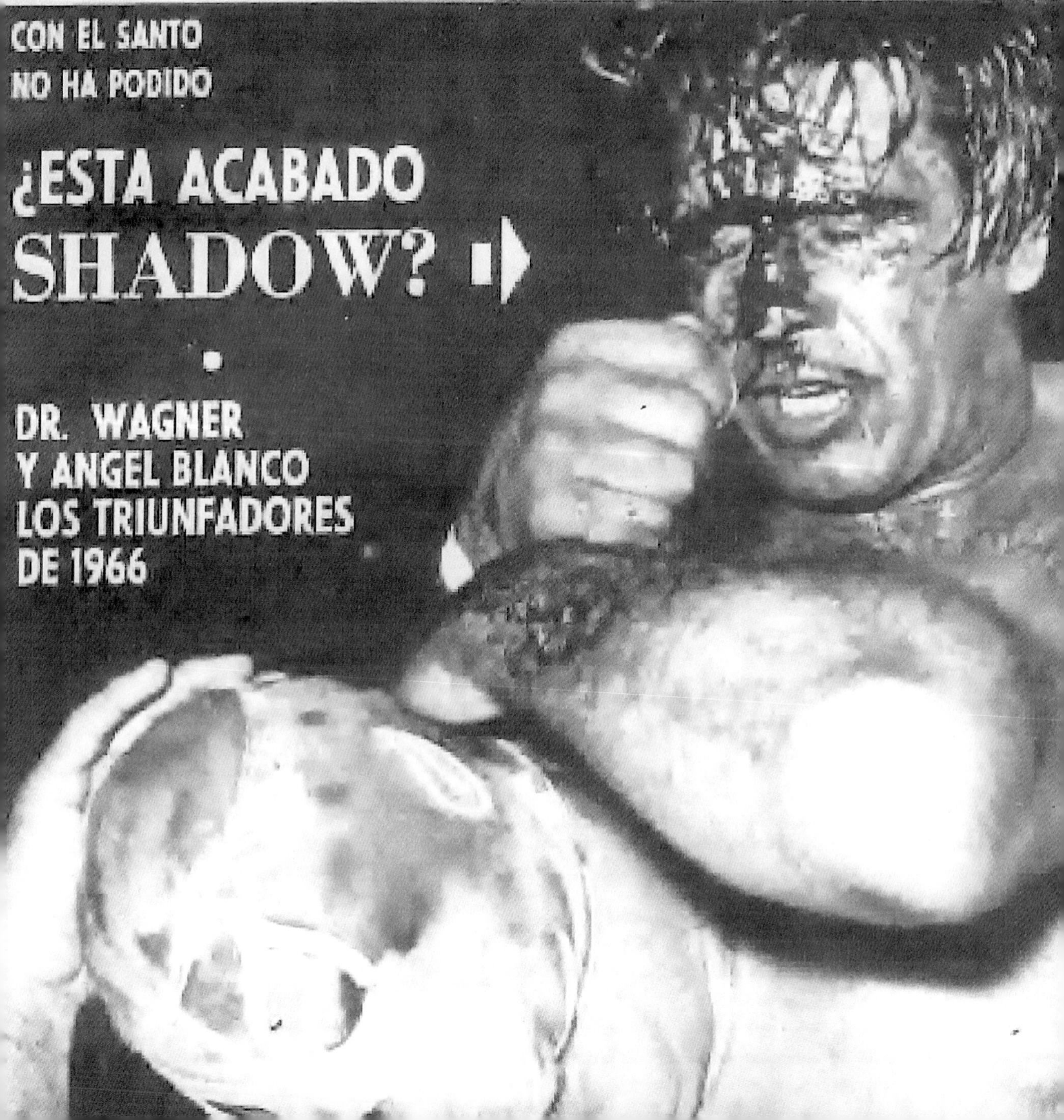

CON EL SANTO
NO HA PODIDO

¿ESTA ACABADO SHADOW? ▷

•

DR. WAGNER
Y ANGEL BLANCO
LOS TRIUNFADORES
DE 1966

biggest names had been his idols. When his music career failed, he joined their ranks. He made his professional debut under the name "Jungla" Cruz, against Rito Romero on June 21, 1942, and lost. Cruz did not like his new ring name. "Jungla" Cruz was a popular character in the funny papers that a local promoter christened him with, but there was nothing funny about the style and competitiveness Cruz would show as the Black Shadow.

Cruz knew that he would have to gain more experience and exposure if he wanted to succeed in the business. He moved to Monterrey and met another extremely colorful character in Lucha: the Blue Demon. He and Demon trained hard and often. Cruz's ring instincts were natural and his athletic abilities were impressive, especially when he started using high-flying moves in his repertoire. With his talent as a Luchador becoming stronger with every outing, Cruz thought it was time to match his ring name to his abilities. The enmascarado Black Shadow was born, with his true identity hidden under a black leather mask. Although his name is Sombra Negra in Spanish, Cruz thought it sounded cooler in English.

Cruz was always a student of physical culture and emphasized stretching in his training regimen (he was a precursor to the Pilates craze of today). He teamed up with his "brother" Blue Demon to start a rudo tag team called Los Hermanos Shadow. The team of Los Hermanos Shadow was a natural to battle the técnico team of La Pareja Atómica. A bitter rivalry developed between both warring teams, which culminated in El Santo against Black Shadow in a máscara contra máscara. After an hour of hard wrestling and high-flying moves, Santo pinned Shadow for the victory.

Fortunately, many viewers found the newly unmasked Black Shadow an entertaining wrestler with his "off-the-top-rope" antics. His popularity increased for a few more years and gained again with his entry into Mexican cinema. But the injuries he accumulated over the years started to take their toll on Shadow's athletic body, and he finally hung up his boots in 1981 after failing to get his wrestling license renewed by the Comisión de Box y Lucha because of ill health. Cruz retired into the shadows (bad pun) and rarely, if ever, grants interviews or talks about his illustrious career as a Lucha Libre superstar.

Cavernario Galindo

With a name like Cavernario (Caveman) Galindo, there's going to be some confusion about one's colorful past. Born, by most accounts, on September 27, 1923, in Chihuahua, Mexico, Cavernario began life as little cave boy Rodolfo Galindo Ramírez, and in his first match in Lucha Libre he debuted in 1938 as Ruddy Valentino under the watchful eye of famed trainer Diablo Velazco. But Cavernario didn't have the natural tools that other Luchadores had when they started out. Galindo was on the skinny side, and that is not the side you want to be on if you want a career in professional wrestling. Cavernario knew this and trained extremely hard—lifting weights and packing quality muscle onto his frame—undergoing a physical transformation, from the scrawny Rodolfo into the brutish Caveman.

Rodolfo wrestled as Ruddy Galindo "El Chacal de Tacubaya" (The Jackal of Tacubaya) early on, when he was still gathering ring experience and honing his mat skills. After winning match after match in smaller venues, Rodolfo found himself in the Mecca of Lucha Libre, the Arena Mexico, and in his match on December 10, 1948, in that hallowed building, he defeated Enrique Llanes. But he wasn't Cavernario yet; he was still Ruddy Galindo. It was Don Salvador Lutteroth himself that renamed Rodolfo Cavernario (Caveman). Now, to be called Cavernario you need to have a few things going for you; in reality, you need to have several things *not* going for you. At the top of that list would be looks. Cavernario's years of hard battles in the ring and a severe car accident at a young age left his face torn and scarred, but he played the ugly Cavernario role to its fullest by honing his wrestling style to reflect his outer appearance. He would kick, punch, bite, choke, bludgeon and bloody his opponents into semiconsciousness. And then as they lay helpless on the mat, he would really give it to them.

A Lucha urban legend circulated about Cavernario taking the "mascot" snake of one of the ring girls and literally tearing it to pieces with his teeth and fingers, like an amped-up circus freak in the ring in front of a completely numbed crowd. This act of alleged animal cruelty for publicity outdates the Ozzy Osbourne dove-eating incident by nearly four decades; our boy Cavernario was such

a trailblazer in the art of repulsive self-promotion that decadent rock stars can't hold a candle to him. His rough and rugged style was the antithesis of the fluid maneuvering of the more highly polished técnicos. He won the Wrestler of the Year award in 1949. Cavernario had some great feuds with Wolf Rubinskis, but his series of "mano a mano" matches (wars) with Gory Guerrero were the stuff legends are made of.

To further fuel the barbaric image he had begun to mold years earlier, Cavernario expressed a cannibalistic urge to actually devour his opponents' flesh. Cavernario would starve himself for a day, building up an unnatural hunger for human meat and then attack and bite his rival. Fans all around Mexico saw Galindo and Guerrero literally rip each other to shreds. Gory was one of the most skilled and technically proficient Luchadores in the business. His style was one that everyone emulated or imitated, but when facing the animalistic Cavernario, all the polish, skill and expertise went out the window as both men engaged in new levels of brutality. Their "SuperLibre" match (a contest that has no count out, no D.Q., and few or any rules) in 1954 is said to be the most vicious and bloodiest confrontation between two Luchadores in Lucha Libre history. Even though Gory beat his out-of-control competitor, he had to go to the hospital for severe blood loss. Cavernario's natural looks led to his portrayal of some villainous characters in films such as *La Bestia Magnífica* (The Magnificent Beast), *Los Tigres del Ring* (Tigers of the Ring), *El Santo contras Las Mujeres Vampiro* (Santo versus the Vampire Women), *Santo en el Museo de Cera* (Santo in the Wax Museum), *Blue Demon contra Los Cerebros Infernales* (Blue Demon versus the Infernal Brains), *Santo el Enmascarado de Plata y Blue Demon contra Los Monstruos* (Santo and Blue Demon versus the Monsters), and the other dozen or so movies he made from the late '50s into the early '70s.

Cavernario was a crowd favorite, not only in his home country but also internationally. But years of brutal abuse to his body led to many nagging injuries that piled up one after another. The unhealthy practice of wrestlers going back into action before they are fully recovered goes on today in both Mexican and American wrestling.

Most, if not all, wrestlers are on painkillers. Wrestling is a business where the adage "out of sight, out of mind" rings true. Wrestlers are afraid to lose their spots on the roster, to lose the heat that they are generating, or to risk being forgotten by the fans.

So Cavernario continued to wrestle up until the mid-seventies. It was then he received an injury that would put him out of commission for good; he broke his vertebra. That was it for the Caveman. He would occasionally wrestle in some small venue but his days of being the ferocious, unpredictable Cavernario were over. He wisely saved and invested the money he made in wrestling and in the movies to buy properties and, like Tarzán, lived a very comfortable post-Lucha life. Cavernario Galindo, the man who thrilled and frightened fans for decades, passed away in Mexico City on July 19, 1999, at age seventy-five.

Diablo Velazco

If there is one name that pops up in the bios of more Luchadores than any other, it is that of Diablo Velazco. "Diablo" was born Cuauhtémoc Velazco Vargas in 1919 in Guadalajara, Jalisco. He took to Lucha like a fish to water when he started wrestling under the guidance of Raúl Romero. After two years of strenuous training under his maestro he-debuted in the ring in 1937 under the name Telmo Velazco. Diablo didn't have the natural size to grow into a bigger wrestler like Luchadores Tarzán López or the Black Shadow. He had a natural tenacity and great skills, but size destined the diminutive Diablo to mid-card status most of his career.

He wrestled for several years but realized his real potential would not be in the ring but behind the scenes. In 1942 he became a trainer, and his infernal reign as Luchador trainer extraordinaire began. In 1959 he became the head trainer of the Arena Coliseo de Guadalajara. The list of wrestlers that Diablo trained is staggering; a partial roll call of luminaries reads: Gory Guerrero, Perro Aguayo, Cavernario Galindo, Bobby Bonales, Atlantis, Cien Caras, Ángel Blanco Sr. and Jr., Tarzán López, Javier "Monarca" Cruz, El Solitario, Rito Romero, Rolando Vera, Hiro Matsuda, Mano Negra, Rayo de Jalisco Sr. and Jr., Solar I and II, and the man of a thousand masks himself, Mil

OPPOSITE: **The tough
team of Ray Mendoza
and René Guajardo**

Máscaras. Like a movie director controlling his actors and action from behind the camera, Diablo trained his protégés and helped build their skills until anyone coming out of the Diablo Velazco training camps was already considered a prospect worth looking out for. A wrestler may have all the heart and desire in the world, but the one factor needed to make him into a champion is a brilliant trainer.

Diablo was a man who went into Lucha not for fame or money, but for his unabashed love of the sport. It was that undying love that kept his energies burning so bright for years. The infectious allegiance he had for Lucha was contagious, for all he trained and everyone who came in contact with him. An old hip injury made him curtail the rigorous training schedule he had for himself and his students. Finally he had to retire from the sport he loved in 1997. Two years later on June 13, 1999, he passed away. The man equated with Lucha Libre excellence was mourned by Luchadores and fans throughout Mexico, but his influence still lives on in the men he trained and the sons of those disciples who carry on the skills Diablo instilled in them years ago.

René Guajardo

Lucha Libre legend René Guajardo was born Juan Manuel Guajardo Mejorado on January 4, 1933, in Villa Mainero, Tamaulipas. His first trainer, Chema López, taught him the basics and brought out Guajardo's natural abilities, but it was the tough Rolando Vera who sharpened and honed his skills to a point where he was noticed by EMLL.

He made his debut for them on October 8, 1954, at the Arena Coliseo. Guajardo started off as a técnico, but after a few years he realized he preferred the jeers to the cheers. He became a rudo and one of the best (or worst) of that time. He hooked up with already popular heel Karloff Lagarde and became one of the premiere rudo tag teams: "Los Rebeldes." Under Lagarde's watchful eye, René's talents as a villain in the ring grew. Soon he became one of the most vilified wrestlers in the business, which is good for the business. And in the true treacherous backstabbing fashion of the rudo, in 1960 René defeated the man who saw so much promise and talent in the youngster, his mentor Rolando Vera, in a match for the NWA World Middleweight. For over a decade he lost and regained that title while battling foes like Antonio Posa, El Rayo de Jalisco, Aníbal and Ray Mendoza. René's sweetest victory was in 1967 against El Santo, to once again win the National Middleweight title.

René and Lagarde may have become sworn enemies in the ring, as all tag teams eventually do, but behind the curtain they were good business partners, along with Ray Mendoza. The trio was the nucleus that helped form the rival UWA. Being the star of this newly formed rival promotion led to victory on November 26, 1975, when he won the first-ever UWA World Middleweight Championship by defeating Aníbal in Mexico City. René started to book his own shows in north Mexico—legend has it that they were on the wild side, even for Lucha Libre. That style of brutal wrestling foreshadowed the ECW hard-core matches of the '90s: chairs, bottles, weapons and foreign objects were all introduced. The fighting outside the ring during the matches was as bloody as the fighting going on inside of it. The atmosphere was laissez-faire at best, and at any moment one felt that the entire building had the potential to erupt in a riot. But if a promotion becomes too complacent and predictable, fans will not think anything of missing a show here and there. But if you keep people guessing and no one knows what type of anarchy might break out, they won't miss out on a spectacular night of entertainment.

René retired from the ring but kept working behind the scenes promoting and booking shows until May 11, 1992, when he succumbed to cancer.

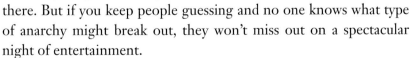

10

"Ya Ain't Seen Nothin' Yet"

The Minis

AS A KID *I was fascinated with midget wrestlers. I thought they were the coolest guys around. Instead of letting society get them down because they weren't like everyone else, they took the road less traveled and joined the hardest fraternity in the world—pro wrestling. Their heart and courage matched anyone who stepped in the ring.*

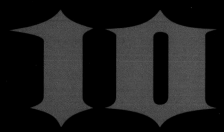

The American "novelty" of midget wrestling in the pro ranks was noticed by the Mexican promoters in the early '50s. They invited some of the wrestlers of smaller physical stature south of the border to work. It wasn't until the seventies, with the advent of Lucha cinema, that

OPPOSITE: The blue Que Monito accompanies the portly Brazo de Plata (Super Porky) into the ring ABOVE: Mini sensation Tsuki leaps after Durango Kid. El Indio is the referee and Jack Black watches from the front row

the midget, or "*mini*" as they are called in Mexico, phenomenon really took off. In several Lucha films midgets or dwarves were used as evil henchmen to the main villain, especially films like *Los Campeones Justicieros* and *Los Vampiros de Coyoacán*. Fans loved the idea of these treacherous little acolytes battling their enmascarados en masse. So if the movie-going public loved it, it only made sense that the Lucha Libre–going fans would enjoy it as well.

The minis that worked in the movies were naturally apt at the physicality that was required in front of the camera, and they took that physical dexterity into the ring. Minis (which is taken from the word *miniestrellas*, little stars) like Gaby Da Silva, Gulliver, Pequeño, Gran Nikolai, and Arturito (named after the tiny droid R2-D2) became popular around the arenas in Mexico. Soon the style of squeezing down full-size Luchadores into mini-versions of themselves started; Mascarita Sagrada was a smaller homage to the real Máscara Sagrada, Octagoncito was a pint-size version of his namesake Octagón. The trend became endless with various vertically challenged clones. One of the most entertaining minis I have seen was a lightning bolt–masked enmascarado named Tsuki; his in-ring work and out-of-ring antics are a real crowd favorite. The minis always bring a new enthusiasm to every card they are on.

Some of the Rest (But Not Even Close To . . .)

There have been so many Luchadores, Luchadoras, minis, exóticos, enmascarados, técnicos, and rudos in the sport's history that to try to give them all equal billing would be virtually impossible. Hundreds and hundreds of wrestlers have stepped into the ring in the last eighty years, from the biggest arenas in Mexico City and around the world to the smallest local venues. Luchadores have entertained and thrilled millions of fans over the decades. Even though we've learned about some of the more famous men and some of the more obscure, I would like to at least put down in print the names of just a few of the men and women who contributed to the history, growth and success of Lucha Libre. In some cases there was not enough information to include everyone on this list, sometimes there were only a few lines about a wrestler's career and at other times only a Luchador's name

could be found in the win/loss column, but they all contributed. Sometimes these people gave just one night or one year and sometimes entire careers, but every aspect was important to the growth and evolution of Lucha. Here is just a partial listing of names that are famous and names that are unknown, but no matter what, they deserve to have their names mentioned: Ringo Mendoza, Volador Jr., Gastón del Valle, La Cebra, Siniestro, Buddy García, Luzbel, Eskimal Jr., Humanungus, Galante, Dragones Chinos, Texano, Corazón de León, Tigre Canadiense, Príncipe Odín, Gran Guerrero, Aníbal, Apolo Dantes, Raúl Torres, Látigo Negro, Gallo Tapado, Matemático, El Comunista, Dick Angelo, Dardo Aguilar, Leopardo, Coloso Colossett, I Mocho Cota, Impala, Zandokan, Diabólica, Troyano, Gallo de Oro, Gárgola, Unicornio, Tony Barbeta, Tirantes, Arkángel, Faraón, Gusano Llanes, Electroshock, Benny Galant, Águila Solitaria, Cibernético, Águila

India, Lizmark Jr., Américo Rocca, Dios de Plata, Gatos Negros, Chico Veloz, Doctor Infernal, El Tapatío, Gárgola, La Cebra, Magia Azul, Pato Salvaje, Ave Blanca, Condorman, Electrón, Ray Valadez, Temojin El Mongol, Black Killer, As Charro, and Luchadoras like Lady Apache, Irma González, and Martha Villalobos.

What's in a Name?

So what's in a name? Everything. In Lucha Libre, when a Luchador or an enmascarado takes on a name other than his real name, he is creating a mystique that will be part of his persona for the rest of his career and eventually his whole life. The monikers, aliases, noms de guerre, or whatever you want to call them become the true identity of the wrestler.

Sometimes promoters will change or give a wrestler his name or the wrestler himself will change his name to something more suitable. Some Luchadores hand down their names to offspring or someone of respect who will carry the name on with honor. Many times a wrestler will go through several name changes in his career until he finds one that suits him, his ring personality, and just as importantly, is a name the fans will accept. The name symbolizes who a wrestler is on the outside as well as on the inside.

Here are just a few of the hundreds of fantastic names Luchadores have chosen. Since I've already talked enough about the big guys, let's give some of the other wrestlers, who are just as important but not as well known outside of Mexico, a little bit of the limelight now. In no particular order, here is a small roll call of some of the more intriguing monikers and what they mean. Both El Sanguinario

and his son El Sanguinario Jr. bear the title Bloodthirsty; I couldn't think of a better name to have in Lucha Libre (or the corporate world). Cien Caras's name means "One Hundred Faces." El Cobarde means the "Cowardly One," and it was such a good name that both brothers became El Cobarde I and II. And if you think Lucha is for the birds, you're right. Here are a few avian aliases that have been popular over the years: Gallo Tapado is the "Covered Rooster," and more than a few eagles have swooped down from the rafters to entertain fans, including Águila Solitaria (Lone Eagle) and Águila de Plata (Silver Eagle). Hawks have gotten their fare share of publicity, like El Halcón (The Hawk) and his son Super Halcón Jr. Then there's Halcón Negro (Black Falcon, no relation).

There was El Egipcio "The Egyptian" and El Faraón "The Pharaoh." And El Santo wasn't the only one named on a spiritual level; there is El Sagrado "The Sacred One" (with the most beautiful mask I think I've seen) and Místico "Mystical." Ángel Mortal is just that—"Deadly Angel," and Arkángel de la Muerte ("Archangel of Death") is a title that sparks fear in people's hearts. One that really hits me is Marabunta ("Ant Plague," which is the name used by the all-consuming massive army of ants in one of the all-time classic short stories "Lennigan vs. the Ants").

El Monstruo pretty well sums it up with his self-explanatory name. And some names just stated the facts on who that Luchador was: La Fiera ("The Fierce"), El Indomable, Violencia, Villanos I to V, El Terrible, Satánico, El Mercenario, Maníaco. No translation needed to get the intent of these guys.

There's been Buccaneers and Gladiators (Bucanero and El Gladiador); foreign-sounding baddies El Chino ("The Chinese One"), El Oriental and Sugi Sito; a whole bunch of supers: Super Astro, Super Boy, Super Caló, Super Comando, Super Kiss, Super Muñeco, Super Niño, Super Parka, Super Pinocho, Super Ratón. A legion of sons and juniors: El Hijo de Aníbal, El Hijo del Diablo, El Hijo del Espanto I, El Hijo del Espanto II, El Hijo del Santo, El Hijo del Solitario, Blue Demon Jr., Lizmark Jr., Dos Caras Jr., Dr. Wagner Jr., Ciclón Veloz Jr., Pierroth Jr., Black Shadow Jr., Emilio Charles Jr., Gran Markus Jr., Karloff Lagarde Jr., Perro Aguayo Jr., and on.

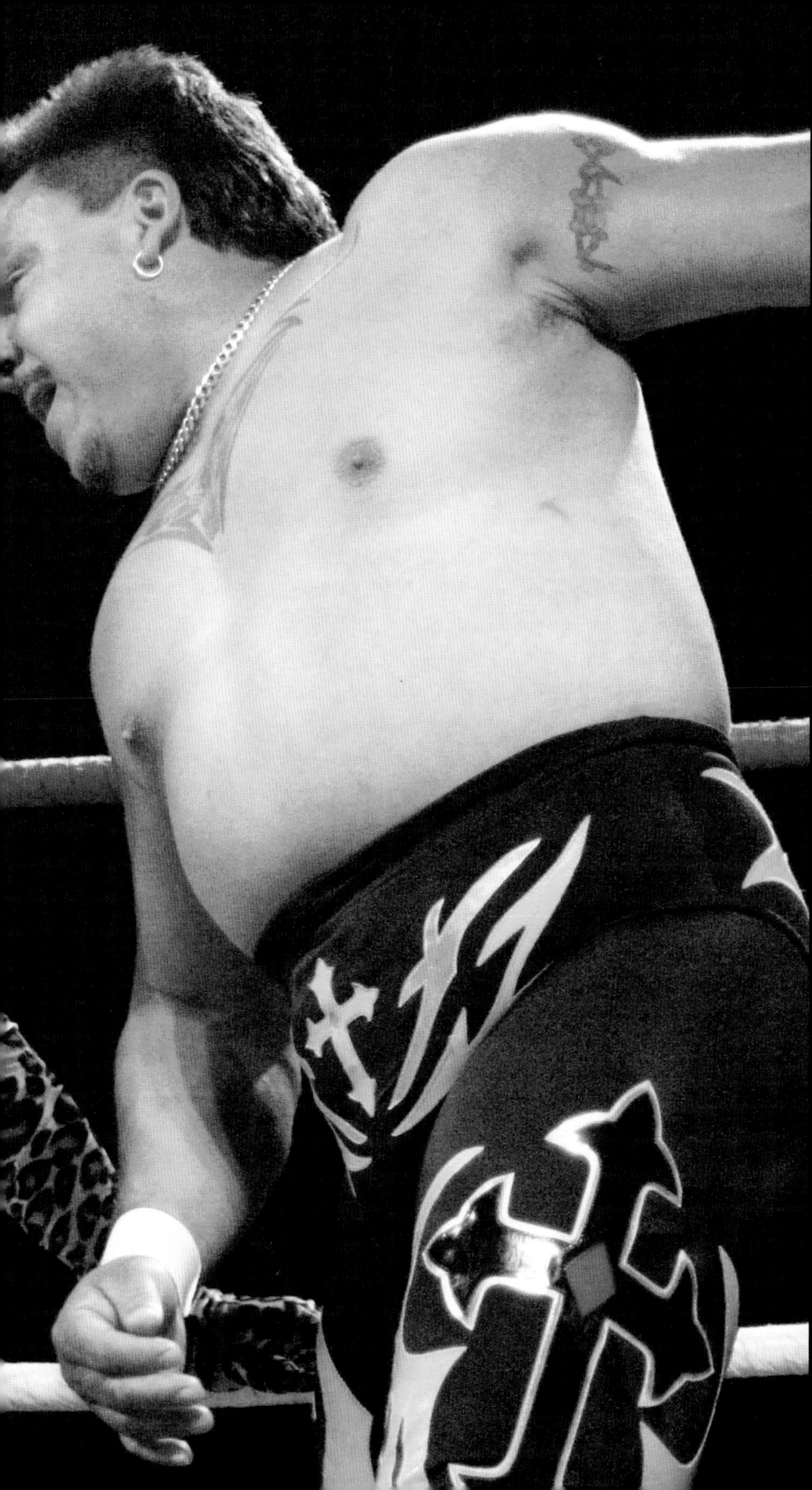

LEFT: Rey Misterio Sr. pummels Mil Máscaras in the corner.

OPPOSITE: "Take that!"

Besides having a really important in-ring name that reflects who you are as an enmascarado or a Luchador, many wrestlers have nicknames that even enhance their reputations and enrich their personas. Everyone in the world who knows El Santo also knows him as "El Enmascarado de Plata" (The Man of the Silver Mask). That name is almost as famous as his ring name. Blue Demon had the nickname "El Manotas" (The Man with the Big Hands), and Mil Máscaras is known as "The Man of a Thousand Masks" or sometimes as "Mr. Personalidad" (Mr. Personality). Aníbal was known as "El Guerrero Cartaginés" (The Carthaginian Warrior) or "La Saeta Azul" (The Blue Arrow); his son El Hijo de Aníbal goes by the nickname "El Hijo de la Saeta Azul" (The Son of the Blue Arrow). Old-school bad-ass Rolando Vera was known as "El Profesor" because everyone he stepped into the ring with, he took to school.

Tinieblas, whose name means "darkness," is also known to many as "El Gigante Sabio" (The Wise Giant); Dr. Wagner, the evil doctor, was known as "El Galeno del Mal," which just happens to mean "The Evil Doctor"; El Solitario was known to his legions of fans as "El Enmascarado de Oro" (The Man of the Golden Mask); Scorpio decided that he would go by the nickname "El Rey Feo" (The Ugly King). His son, Scorpio Jr., may have loved his father's ring name but he went the polar opposite when it came to his nickname, which is "El Guapo" (The Handsome One); the great Blue Panther is known as "El Maestro Lagunero" (The Lagoon Master); there is a little colorful confusion between Loco Zandokan, who is known as "El Rudo de los Ojos Esmeralda" (The Rudo with the Emerald Eyes), and El Dandy, whose similar moniker is "El Rudo de los Ojos Verdes" (The Green-eyed Rudo); Gran Markus was known as "El Gigante de la Laguna" (Lagoon Giant); Black Gordman was a rose by another name when he was called "El Diablo Rojo" (The Red Devil); the Black Shadow was "El Príncipe Negro" (Black Prince); Felino's name belied his talent "El Luchador Más Rápido" (The Fastest Luchador); Sangre Chicana (Chicano Blood) was "El Amo del Escándalo" (The King of Scandals).

The Lee Falk comic strip "The Phantom" inspired Fantasma who goes by "El Duende que Camina" (The Walking Ghost); the

demonic Damián 666 has a more than appropriate alias in "La Bestia del Apocalipsis" (The Apocalypse Beast); green-and-yellow clad enmascarado Fishman was also called "El Látigo Lagunero" (The Lagoon Whip); Mr. Niebla (Mr. Fog) has a rather fanciful alter-ego name "El Caballero del Estilo Diferente" (The Gentleman with a Different Style); Chessman is known as "El Asesino de la Luz Roja" (The Red Light Assassin). The crafty Lizmark was known to his fans as "El Geniecillo Azul" (The Little Blue Genie); Firpo Segura doesn't pull any punches when he tells everyone that he is "El Rey del Derechazo" (The King of the Right Hand Punch); legendary Enrique Llanes was "El Sol de Otumba" (Otumba's Sun); Shu El Guerrero was also known by his diabolic nickname "El Guerrero del Averno" (Warrior from Hell). This one makes one scratch his head: Máscara Año 2000 goes by the overly paternal handle "El Padre de Más de 20" (The Father of More Than 20—I wonder what Mrs. Mother of More Than 20 did with her spare time); Silver King had twin nicknames "El Fabuloso" (The Fabulous One) and "El Efectivo" (The Effective One); the cool-looking skeletal L. A. Park has a bony nickname "La Calaca" (Skeleton of Death); the intensely high-flying Super Crazy is called "The Insane Luchador"; Espectro I had the viridian name "El Hombre Verde" (The Green Man); pit-bull tough multititle holder Perro Aguayo was feared as the ferocious "El Can de Nochistlán" (The Dog from Nochistlán); Carlos Alvarado González wrestled as Bobby Lee but was also noted as being "El Enmascarado Verde" (The Green Maskman) and "La Bestia del '78" (The Beast of '78); Tinieblas Jr. has been called "El Hijo del Gigante Sabio" (The Son of the Wise Giant) by many; Volador Jr. has the aerial nickname "El Novato del Aire" (The Flying Novice); Jaque Mate (Checkmate, get it?) has the nickname "El Hombre de la Jugada Mortal" (The Man with the Deadly Movement). Los Hermanos Espanto went by "Los Sustos" (The Scares); Mogur was called "El Gato Egipcio" (The Egyptian Cat); the always entertaining Cassandro is gladly known as "Queen of the Ring," and fellow exótico Pimpinela Escarlata has the royal moniker of "La Primera Dama de la Lucha" (The First Lady of Wrestling), and the eye candy Tarzan Boy is sexily known by his female fans as "El Consentido de las Damas" (The Pampered One by the Ladies).

The Future of Lucha . . .

So many of the Luchadores and enmascarados performing today are incredible. The talent that is being drawn into the ranks from Mexico and parts of Southern California and Southern Texas is really something to behold. Recently I saw a young enmascarado named Místico perform in Los Angeles; when he would fly out of the ring and soar across the ropes at his opponents, you'd swear he had the ability to alter the time/space relationship just like the slo-mo action scenes in the *Matrix* movies. Gravity has nothing on him. And he is just one of a whole new generation that have started to look and study the fantastic aerial feats and ring supremacy of the enmascarados that have come before them.

It is evolution at its finest, every subsequent generation growing stronger and more capable than their predecessors'. They wrestle in the famous arenas and all the unknown locations. They wrestle all over Mexico and Southern Texas and in places in California like the famous Olympic or the Forum or neighborhood venues in East L.A. or El Monte or Bakersfield. Places like the Fairgrounds in Indio or in Compton in the Youth Athletic League or the Crystal Park Casino. They wrestle all over the world, wherever a promoter will pay for their talents or, more importantly, wherever fans eagerly wait to watch them perform. Luchadores were born to wrestle and are destined to roam. One must have taste for the road as well as a hunger for the

ring. The Luchador is never one to stay in a single place for too long. There is always another match somewhere out there to be fought.

The quality of this generation is something to marvel, men like Último Guerrero (Last Warrior), Perro Aguayo Jr., Héctor Garza, Juventud Guerrera, Psicosis, (sometimes spelled Psychosis in America) and Super Crazy are just a few of the next generation of superstars. Guerrera, Psicosis and Super Crazy have all entered the ranks of mainstream American wrestling as a rebellious Mexican trio called the "Mexi-cools," who drive around on John Deere lawn mowers, drink beer and carry around a piñata. The lone enmascarado who is a true standout in American wrestling today is Rey Mysterio Jr., a highly gifted and outstanding wrestler whose amazing in-ring abilities are only matched by his out-of-ring class.

A Family Affair

Welcome to the family business that is Lucha Libre. The world of Lucha is so compelling and alluring that it is almost impossible for the offspring of Luchadores to walk away from what has been a family tradition and honor. So many Luchadores come from long family lines of Lucha Libre greats. Enmascarados tend to will their masks to their children; fathers have passed down their personas to sons, uncles to nephews, brothers to brothers. There is a continuity of character that keeps ring personas a legacy of the previous owner's unique personality and an extension of the heirs. The man may be dead but the myth lives on; El Santo is gone but his son not only carries on as the heir apparent to ring royalty but he has become his father's alter ego. It is not only masked men who have family members that follow them up the stairs and into the ring. Just take a look below at the tangled branches of the Lucha Libre family tree.

We already know the late Eddie Guerrero's father was the legendary Gory Guerrero, whose other sons are Chavo, Mando, Hector and grandson Chavo Jr., who have all entered the world of Lucha Libre. Also in that family was Enrique Llanes (Enrique Juan Yañez González), the former National Light Heavyweight title and NWA World Middleweight title, who was Eddie's uncle by marriage; his son Javier Llanes, CMLL World Middleweight title, was Eddie, Mando, Chavo and Héctor's cousin. Fabled Luchador Ray Mendoza had five sons who all went into the family business as Los Villanos (I, II, III, IV, V). Tinieblas begat Tinieblas Jr. Black Guzmán's brother was the one and only El Santo, who begat Hijo del Santo. Not to be outdone, Blue Demon did some begetting of his own and came up with Blue Demon Jr. Místico's father is Dr. Karonte, his brother is Astro Boy I, and Tony Salazar is his uncle. Juventud Guerrera's father was multiple title holder Fuerza Guerrera. The more than ample Super Porky's father was Shadito Cruz; Porky's sons are Máximo and Kronos; his brothers are the renowned Los Brazos: Brazo de Oro, El Brazo, Brazo Cibernético, Super Brazo, Brazo de Platino; his nephew is La Máscara, and La Alimaña is a brother-in-law. Príncipe Odín's sons are Super Comando, Artillero and Sombra de Plata. Negro Casas's father is Pepe Casas; his brothers are Felino and Heavy Metal; his brother-in-law is Veneno, and his cousin wrestles as Black Star. Perro Aguayo's son Perro Aguayo Jr. also wrestles; his brother-in-law is El Ídolo; his sons, Perro's nephews are Los Ídolos I and II, and Pepe Aguayo II. Pierroth Jr.'s brother is El Incógnito but Pierroth Sr. is not his father. Rey Misterio's nephew is Rey Mysterio Jr. Rayo de Jalisco Jr.'s dad is Ray de Jalisco Sr., and his son is Ray de Jalisco #2 (which, in reality, makes him #3), who also wrestled under the name Rayman; his cousins are Úabra Rayo, Mr. Rayo, and Rayo Star, and Luchadores Tony Sugar and Black Sugar are his uncles. René Guajardo had only one son (luckily) and he wrestled as . . . you guessed it, René Guajardo Jr. Huracán Ramírez's brothers are Catedrático, Ruddy García, and El Demonio Rojo; his nephews are El Matemático and Huracán Jr. but El Matemático's sons are Matemático Jr. (sometimes known as Libertador), Matemático II (who is known at times as Turbina) and Matemático III (who is just

Psicosis (sometimes spelled Psychosis just to keep life complicated) has a brother named Fobia who wrestles. Ángel Blanco had an angelic brood called Los Hijos del Ángel Blanco I and II, plus another son called Ángel Blanco Jr. as well as an ex-son-in-law who went by the Ángel Blanco Jr. moniker for a while before one of his real sons took it over. El Espectro's sons are Hijo del Espectro and El Picudo; his nephews are El Espectro Jr., Cadaver de Ultratumba and Guerrero de la Muerte. Tough Rolando Vera's nephew is wrestler Alex Romano. Lizmark has a son named Lizmark Jr. and a brother named Lizmark II (glad to see the Lizmarks have as much originality in their family as the Ángel Blancos). Héctor Garza's father was Humberto Garza; his brother is Humberto Garza Jr. and his uncle is Mario Segura. Scorpio had a little stinger named Scorpio Jr. Mil Máscaras's brothers are Sicodélico and Dos Caras, so naturally his nephews are Sicodélico Jr. and Dos Caras Jr.; the elder Sicodélico's brother-in-law is Black Gordman, and his stepson is Black Gordman Jr.

Bestia Salvaje's father was Espectro II (not Espectro I, that would be too easy); his brother is Corazón Salvaje and his brother-in-law is Charrito de Oro. Rey Halcón's son is Mephisto. Rey Bucanero's uncles are Pirata Morgan, Hombre Bala and Verdugo. Apolo Dantés's father was Alfonso Dantés; his brother is Cesar Dantés; Septiembre Negro is a great-uncle; Al Amezcua was his grandfather and Alberto Muñoz and Indio Jerónimo are uncles. Super Parka (who used to wrestle under the name Volador) has a son named Volador Jr.; one of his nephews is the *original* La Parka (not that fake La Parka we learned about earlier) and another nephew is Suplex; Johnny Ibarra and El Desalmado are his brothers, which makes them Volador Jr.'s uncles. The mighty massive Canek has two sons who are named El Hijo Del Canek and Canek Jr. (come on, isn't that practically the same thing?); at least Canek's brothers had some variation to their choice of names, Príncipe Maya and El Danés I. Dr. X (and you have to dig that name) had three sons, one named El Cobarde and I'm sure he figured "what the hell, let's name the other one something easy to remember" so the second son went by the name El Cobarde II; the third son was known as Convoy and changed his name to Legendario, but finally decided on the familiar El Cobarde Jr, just to confuse everyone. El Cobarde

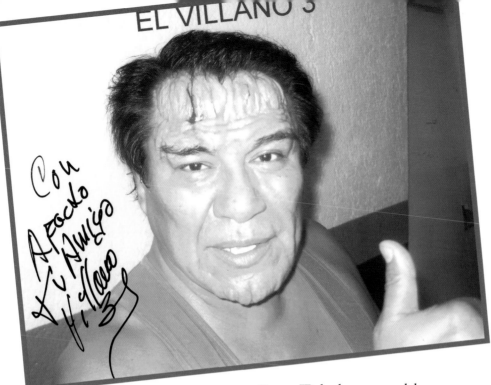

EL VILLANO 3

Con
A focto
y Amigo
Villano III

(I not II) had a son and he named him El Hijo del Cobarde Jr. (figures). The famous Karloff Lagarde had a brother named El Ángel Negro and a nephew named Karloff Lagarde Jr.

Now it gets really mind-blowing. The infamous trio Los Hermanos Espanto weren't all real brothers. Espanto I (José Eusebio Vázquez Bernal) and Espanto III (Miguel "Miguelito" Vázquez Bernal) were real-life siblings, but Espanto II (Fernando Cisneros Carrillo) wasn't blood-related, however, he was so close to Espanto I that he considered him a real brother and so will we; Espanto IV and Espanto V are the sons of Espanto III (which makes them Espanto I's nephews); Los Hijos del Espanto I and II are considered the "ring sons" of Espanto II (the non-blood-related Espanto), but there is no blood lineage—just the shared ring name; then there is Espanto Jr. (Jesús Andrade Salas, who happens not to be related to anyone who shows up above and I still don't know where he came from, but he has two real-life brothers: Sergio and César Andrade Salas), who wrestles as—you got it—Hijos del Espanto; and if that isn't enough to drive you crazy, there is a midget wrestler who goes by the mini version name of El Espantito.

So You Wanna Be a Luchador?

You think you're up for it? You're in good shape, you have a background in martial arts—wrestling, maybe judo. You have pretty good stamina, you're naturally athletic and flexible. That's all well and good but it is not even going to get you into a "prelim" match. To become a Luchador is a commitment, the complete surrendering of your will and soul to Lucha. Before you think about surrendering those, you better find yourself a *Maestro* (trainer). He will teach you what you will need to carry you down the hard and arduous road, but even that doesn't guarantee success.

Luchadores must have the same spark that sumo wrestlers and prizefighters have, a spark that will build and burn into a fiery passion and keep them warm on those long and cold nights on the road. There is no such thing as half-assed in Lucha; you do everything 110%. Maestros are very leery when they encounter someone off the street who comes into their gym asking to train to become a Luchador. It all sounds easy and fun but once you hit the mat for your first training session, it will not take long to separate the boys from the men, and then the men from the potential Luchadores.

There is a custom that the first time on the mat for a novice determines if they have what it takes. Be prepared to be extremely sore for a long time after your first training in the Lucha style. And if you can take the physical pounding that you will receive and come back the next day for some more, there is no pat on the back or prize. That is merely the minimum of what is expected of you. I went down to watch some Luchador hopefuls train at the New Japan Dojo in Santa Monica. The class was taught by two of the top Luchadores in the business today, the Durango Kid and Chilango. Both men are in phenomenal shape and it was evident as they led their class through an hour of nonstop calisthenics and wrestling moves. Then there was an hour of practicing moves, tosses and throws and landings. Then some more running, calisthenics and stretching. I was tired just watching them warm up.

But even strenuous training doesn't guarantee you will get work. One Luchador named Junior—who goes by the name "Fabulous Hernández," and has wrestled pro for a couple of years and still

SOUVENIR WRESTLING MASKS

by Keith J. Rainville

In the U.S., black T-shirts are the typical souvenir for wrestling fans, but not so south-of-the-border. In Mexico, it's all about the replica mask. Outside of arenas on fight night, vendors set up blankets and makeshift display racks loaded with cheap (but functional) copies of the masks worn both by stars of the day and legends of the past. They are especially popular with kids, and you'll see hundreds if not thousands of these worn in the stands by fans supporting their ring idols.

The masks are cheap, made of a baffling array of outré Mexican textiles. Remnants of sequined gown materials and recycled auto upholstery abound. The masks are unlicensed, but the enmascarados face the copyright violations with a certain zen. The tradition goes back decades, and while they may not be especially thrilled to autograph a pirated copy of their mask, they must get a rush looking out from the ring at a cheering crowd littered with copies of their hoods.

Souvenir masks started floating into the States as an underground import with the Internet boom of the nineties. By now, they are all over eBay and show up as kitsch in trendy boutiques. This has posed a new problem for the scorned enmascarado, as pirated bootlegs of their masks are used by Yanks from backyard wrestlers to indie filmmakers to surf and punk bands. Isolated from their original cultural context, the replica masks are often assumed to be "generic" designs and used without regard.

Now, before you go buy one of these for your kid at Halloween, keep in mind these are not made to any type of garment safety specifications. The materials, and especially the glues, used can be flammable. They're not tailored to your head, either, so expect skin irritation and an itchy scalp.

Some of the finer mask artisans in Mexico, and even a few in the U.S. offer high-quality custom commissions that rival the real deal. The finest of the lot are from the originators of

the Lucha mask, Deportez Martínez in Mexico City, and the renowned Cacao Planning artists in Japan. Another great by-product of Lucha Libre's inroads into the U.S. is big stars doing autograph signings here. They often sell their ring-worn hoods, the most prized being ones ripped to shreds and stained with the dried blood of previous battles. The elite ring-worn mask collector doesn't mind shelling out $300 to $500 for such a piece of ring history. 💀

ABOVE: Just a few of Keith Rainville's Lucha Libre masks from his extensive collection

trains with Durango and Chilango—sums up how hard the life is: "There are times I take matches for so little money that at times it barely covers the cost of gas to get to the venue." It is not just a hard life; it is an existence that no one outside of the business will be able to relate to. You become a nomad, a traveling knight errant always on a quest. You never stay in one place too long; there is always another show in another town on a different night. The closest thing you can compare it to is being in a rock band: The daily grind and nightly shows take a cumulative toll on your body, mind and soul after years on the road. You don't get a weekly paycheck; you get paid for the shows you work in. And don't think you are going to spend a lot of time with your family; that is, if you ever had the time to start a family. You miss birthdays, anniversaries, births, funerals. When they say the show must go on, it goes on, and you better be ready to perform.

And as I list all the negative aspects of the lifestyle (but not the sport), I can still feel the pull myself. I can see how the odyssey of the open road and adventures in the ring would be a siren's call beckoning the young and enthusiastic to venture into the mysterious world of overcrowded arenas, boisterous crowds, epic battles and nightly victories.

Let's say you've gone to a Maestro, you've trained hard, your skills are sharpened, your ring abilities are solid and your trainer thinks you're ready for your first match. You've dreamed about this day, the moment you can put on a mask and go out and entertain the crowd. Guess what? Unless you pass the physical inspection by the Commission of Lucha Libre and their examination of your skills and talent, it will not happen.

The commission is part of the Federal District (originally Comisíon de Box y Lucha Libre). This commission has been around as long as Lucha has been in Mexico and was originally a branch of the Oficina de Espectáculos Públicos. The commission regulates everything to do with Lucha Libre in Mexico, from Luchadores' licenses to physicals, to assigning referees to handing out disciplinary actions if needed. The commission in Mexico for wrestling is more stringent than it is for boxing in most of the United States.

The men on the commission have been involved with Lucha Libre for years; some have spent lifetimes behind the scenes or in the ring. Many a famous former Luchador left the ring to sit on the board of the commission, and you can be guaranteed that they will not just hand out a wrestling license to just anyone who wants one. There is a time-honored tradition of excellence in Lucha. Even if you're very talented and have good skills, that still isn't good enough—you must be excellent. The commission will not give anyone the chance to embarrass or bring shame to their profession. After years of training (and it is years), you must go before a certifying board to pass a very strenuous test of your skills and abilities. If you should pass, don't think it gets any easier; every two years you get tested again.

No one is allowed to sit on their laurels. Being a Luchador is excruciatingly difficult and becoming an enmascarado is even harder. Máscaras are just not handed out willy-nilly. The commission is even harder on candidates who want to try out to be enmascarados, because just having a sword doesn't make you a samurai, and having a mask doesn't make you an enmascarado. When a Luchador receives his mask, his lifestyle changes the moment that mask covers his face. Rudo and técnico alike live by the same code. You must never do anything that would bring shame or dishonor to the code of the enmascarado or bring shame to Lucha. An enmascarado must never take his mask off in public, ever! He must never let his identity be known to the masses. There are rules about who can know your identity (family, close friends, tag team partners), rules about when and where you can take your mask off.

You may NOT pull or tear off the mask of your opponent (although rudos do this to build heat). If you should have your mask pulled off, you must cover your face with your hands (or someone throws you a towel), but you cannot keep wrestling unless you have the chance to retrieve your mask and put it back on. The ideology there is that it is better to take a sound thrashing than to have your true self revealed.

There is no indecision on staying incognito. Ring announcer Gasparín, "the voice of Lucha Libre in California," conveyed a story that exemplifies the tradition of keeping one's identity a secret. He wrestled as an enmascarado but kept his ring persona secret from even his own kids. One day he found himself at the Lucha Libre matches watching the show with his family, sitting ringside. The promoter of the show was in a bind because one of the stars of the main event was a no-show and he needed a quick substitute to complete the tag team. The promoter knew Gasparín well and knew his past and practically begged him to give him a hand. Gasparín told his family he had to speak to some friends backstage and he hurried home, pulled out his mask and trunks, went back to the venue and entered through the back door. He suited up and went out for the main event as a rudo against a técnico tag team. They had a wild match and Gasparín found himself being tossed out of the ring and literally at the feet of his kids, who were jeering at him, pointing their fingers and cursing, the rudo.

Gasparín, trying not to laugh, chided his own kids for speaking to him that way. The kids froze when he called them by name. Gasparín slid back into the ring and continued the match with his kids standing in shock, not knowing what had happened. Afterward he showered quickly and met his kids as the last match was ending. They couldn't wait to tell their absent dad what happened to them. He still laughs about it today.

Oooh-La-La . . . Masks, Muscles, and Mischief

What is better than watching a wrestling card full of skilled Luchadores flying around the ring, giving it their all, battling from the opening bell to the ref's final count? Watching a wrestling card full of skilled Luchadores flying around the ring, giving it their all, battling from the open bell to the ref's final count . . . with scantily clad, gyrating women shaking their more than ample wares between the matches. If that sounds appealing, *mi hermanos*, say hello to "Lucha VaVoom"—a cross-culture pollination of the finest exports of two countries: Mexican Lucha Libre and good ol' American burlesque.

It was a natural marriage—Lucha has always had a long-standing tradition of entertainment, physical perfection, athletic prowess and audience participation. Burlesque has all that plus the lovely

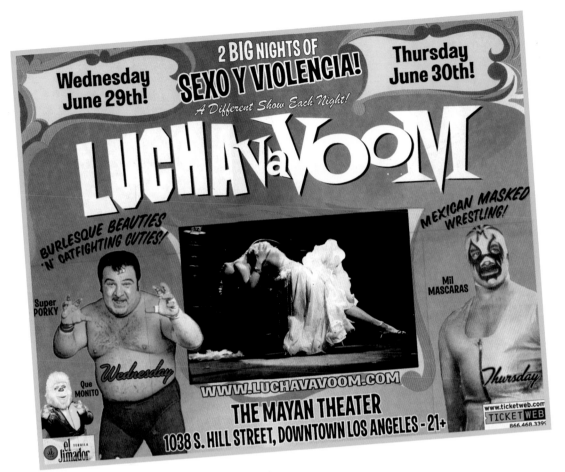

ABOVE: **A poster from Lucha VaVoom with two Luchadores from opposite ends of the physically fit spectrum: Super Porky and Mil Máscaras**

ladies. Lucha VaVoom is a crazy hybrid of high flying and high jinks that takes place several times a year at the Mayan Theater in downtown Los Angeles. The show has been going on for several years now. It started, like most cult favorites, as a word-of-mouth experience that had to be seen to be believed.

The ingredients for such a successful cocktail are one part Lucha Libre, with participants from Mexico and Southern California who already have a huge fan base, and one part the shapely ecdysiast specialists from the L.A./Hollywood scene who came out of the former burlesque troupe "The Velvet Hammer." Throw in a few minis, a couple of comics, a guy on a pogo stick, an eye-catching trannie and an audience full of hipsters. Shake well, pour over a rocks glass and enjoy (small paper umbrella is optional).

By far the best ring entrance at Lucha VaVoom was Cassandro's. He dressed as a nun, and somber Gregorian chants played over the speakers as two white-robed monks led him to the ring. As soon as he

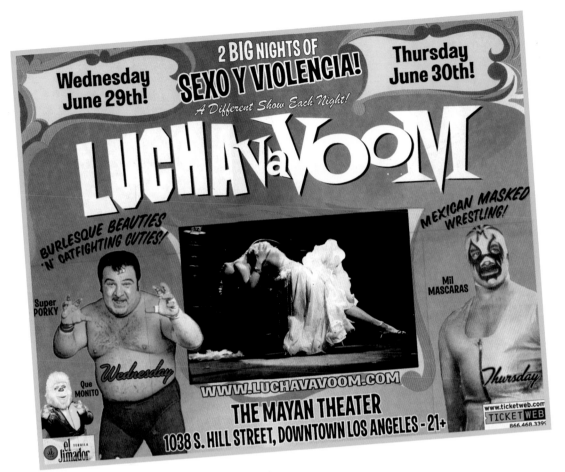

WED OCT. 29 · MAYAN
1038 S. Hill St. Downtown LA · doors

Monster
his Match

La Parka

Vampire
Women

LUCH

HALLO

Live
Mexican Masked Wrestling

THEATER
30 | show 8:00

Na Voom

WEEN SHOW

with Mil Mascaras!

Huracan Ramirez, Jr.
Batwoman,
Crazy Chickens
& much, much more!

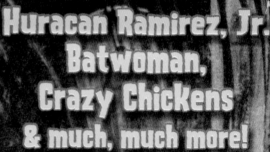

tickets available at:
WACKO, BRAT, &
HOLLYWOOD BOOK & POSTER,
or on the web at:
WWW.TICKETWEB.COM

Live Mexican Wrestl

Burlesque & Com

Lucha VaV

Valentin LOV

Mucho mas SEXO y VIOLENCIA!!!!

Directamente de Mexico!

he Space Cadets,
SOLAR, SUPER ASTRO & ULTRAMAN!

Spectacular battle of the minis!,
with MASCARITA SAGRADA,
TSUKI, PIRATITA MORGAN
& GUERRERITO DEL FUTURO

with hosts
Patton Oswalt &
Blaine Capatch

1038

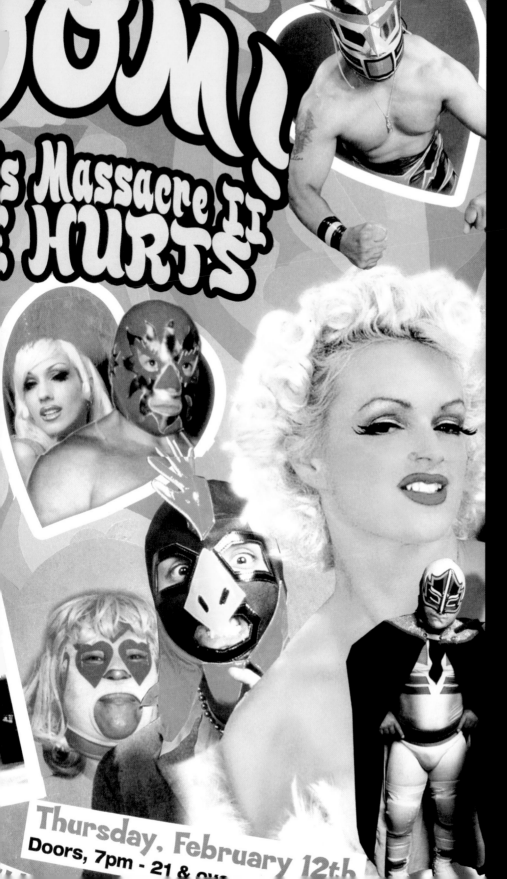

hit the front stage, the music burst into a hot Latin number, and Cassandro stripped down to a black leather corset and fishnets and put on one hell of a show. No hang-ups, no attitude, just lots of fun. For years Lucha Libre has had two characters in its ranks: the técnico and the rudo, the good guy and the bad guy. Cassandro is a new breed of Luchador that has recently come to the forefront: the *exótico*. The exóticos have been around for years but only now are they getting the big push. In a world of high testosterone and centuries of machismo, the exótico is a new wrinkle on the battle-scarred masks of Lucha. Overly flamboyant, feminine and sexually ambiguous, the exótico is a wrestler who at times fascinates the crowd as well as confuses their opponents with their ring attire, and hyper histrionics.

But there is nothing soft about these charismatic competitors.

Even though they look like they robbed Liberace's closet, these Luchadores are just as tough as their excessively manly counterparts. Behind the multicolored feather boas, beneath the sequins and pasties, beyond the makeup and lipstick, burns the heart of the classically trained Luchador.

Just as the black mask is an extension of the dark side of the rudo and the white mask echoes the purity of the técnico, the exótico's glitzy and showy persona is the extension of their vibrant personalities. And just because some may swish and sway into the ring, do not take that as a sign of weakness. At a recent Lucha VaVoom show Cassandro performed every night with a perforated intestine, two broken ribs and a swollen ankle; not many athletes can do that. When I asked him why he would go on that night with all those injuries, his answer surprised me. "With all the discomfort I am going through, once I step in front of that crowd and hear those fans cheer, every ounce of pain vanishes. Performing is my medicine. Lucha is my life."

The crowds at the Lucha VaVoom shows are the complete polar opposites of the crowds that attended the Lucha shows in Compton and South Central. Even though most of the Luchadores on the VaVoom card will wrestle the next night in these cities after they have wrestled in the Mayan,

ABOVE: The Durango Kid has one of the Poubelle Twins just where he wants her

LEFT: The toughest Luchador in a feathered headpiece, the always beautiful and always dangerous Queen of the ring, Cassandro, *exótico* extraordinaire

I have yet to see anyone from the VaVoom shows except the performers themselves show up at any of these performances. Lucha VaVoom is one of those things unique to Los Angeles. Although it is moving across the country to places like Chicago and Las Vegas, it is truly an L.A. creation. The crowds at VaVoom are the neo-retro-hipsters-beatniks-pre-post-punk-slackers. Ninety percent of the audience is Anglo at a VaVoom show, and yet ninety-eight percent of the crowds at any other South California show are Mexican; the other two percent are usually me and my photographer.

Keith Rainville, Eddie Mort, and Christa Faust also regularly show up at all the Lucha matches. Keith is the publisher of *From Parts Unknown*, a great magazine that is the only cool Lucha Libre–themed publication aimed for the Anglo fans as well as the Mexican fans—he is also the guy who coined the term "Lucha VaVoom." Eddie Mort and Lili Chin are the co-creators of the hit animated series *Mucha Lucha*, a favorite of kids and adults. Author Christa Faust wrote the first and coolest Lucha Libre noir crime novel, *Hoodtown*, a delicious combination of sexy zaftig female enmascarados and hard-boiled prose. Her style of writing and storytelling has led to the birth of a new genre in fiction. Along with Rafael Navarro's great graphic novel and comic creation, *El Sonámbulo*, a throwback to the old-school pulp characters, these two writers have created the masked Lucha detective hero genre. (Two other interesting Lucha-themed comics are the Charles Burns creation *El Borah* and Jamie and Gilbert Hernández's (also known as Los Bros Hernández) great comic called *Whoa Nellie!* about female Mexican wrestlers.)

These artists see what Lucha is, a venue to express one's inner creativity, if not in the ring than by its guiding influence. Several leading and emerging artists have used the

OPPOSITE: Rosa Salvaje readies for in-ring action

BELOW: Blue Demon guest-stars on the hit animated show *¡Mucha Lucha!*

Lucha Libre tableaux as a starting point to express their works.

Up-and-coming gallery star Antonio Pelayo uses Latino portraiture. His depiction of El Santo created a recent buzz when it was revealed that the entire piece was done with just a number two pencil. Andrew Barr's kick-ass web comic "Beach Blanket Bloodbath" and his comic books "Something a Go-Go" showcase some great artwork and stories. The twisted brain trust behind Muttpop, Inc., Robert Silva and Jerry Frissen, have created a fantastic comic book/animated series/toy line called Luchadores 5 that is a new departure for Lucha characters as well as for the fans.

Even Rob Zombie is getting into the act by producing an animated feature with Lucha characters. Not to be outdone, Hollywood finally realized that there was money to be made in the masked wrestling genre, and the hit Jack Black vehicle *Nacho Libre* (based on a true story of a Catholic priest who moonlighted as an enmascarado to raise money for his poor parish—the true story is more amazing than the Tinseltown adaptation) was released in the summer of 2006.

Even the music scene has been touched by the Lucha craze. A group out of Canada called The Tijuana Bibles dons Lucha masks when they hit the stage. No group comes close to Los Straitjackets, an incredible Lucha/surf/instrumental band. Wearing complete Lucha gear, these guys grind away on tour all year long. Southern Culture on the Skids is a rock group out of the south that tears up the stage with backwoods intensity. Having grown up on cheap whiskey, raucous rock 'n' roll and Santo movies, they even have some of their

OPPOSITE: The incredible Cassandro in mid-flight, about to land on the Durango Kid (Jack "Nacho Libre" Black is in the back in mid-clap)

ABOVE: For a double-barreled barrage of cool music and hot shows, check out Lucha-influenced Los Straitjackets' live performances

albums covered in Luchado imagery. Even the Lucha Libre film is making a comeback in genre starlet director Jeff Burr's feature *Mil Máscaras vs. the Aztec Mummy*—a good old-fashioned slice of masked mayhem for another generation to appreciate.

And what book about Lucha Libre would be complete without at least a passing nod to the *numero uno* Lucha Libre fan Johnny Legend. You have to know Johnny to really get a feel for the guy; words and descriptions can't quite cut it. With his trademark flowing white beard and an unquenchable thirst for the bizarre in life, Johnny has seen and done it all in the underbelly of Hollywood. Known by many as the Rockabilly Rasputin, he has been a singer, an actor and a wrestling promoter, and the number-one advocate of pushing El Santo and the Lucha Libre films in the seventies when no one in the country other than K. Gordon Murray and a select handful knew about these things.

Lucha on the Newsstands

The media of Mexico respects Lucha Libre far more than the American media does. Every time a professional wrestler or a certain promotion is mentioned in the American news, it is always followed with a smirk or a sly wink to the camera, as if the newscaster is in on a joke that no one else knows. There is a condescending attitude toward pro wrestling in the states, whether it happened when pro wrestling stopped calling itself a sport and became "sports entertainment" or whether the crowds became too sophisticated, the media, newspapers, magazines, and broadcast news only report on the spectacle that surrounds the sport, and not the matches themselves. There are magazines that cover just the world of pro wrestling and websites that keep their finger on the pulse of the business, but no mainstream publication or periodical would ever entertain the idea of reporting on the action inside the squared circle. Not the case in Mexico. Respectable mainstream newspapers like *L'Afición* and *Ovaciones* report aspects of Lucha Libre, from matches to the unmasking of an enmascarado.

Some of the oldest magazines to cover Lucha have become collector's items. In the past, three of the best-known publications to

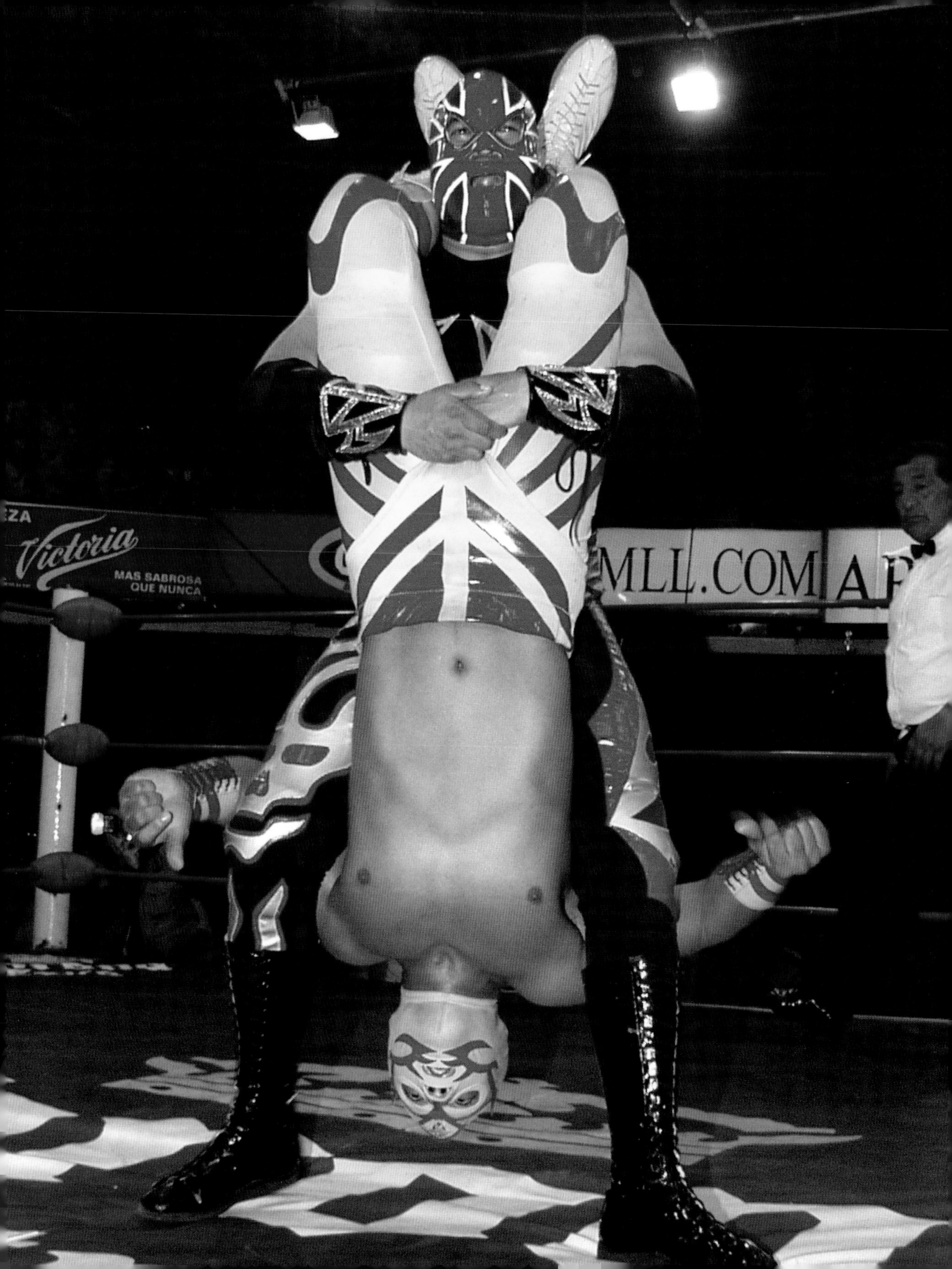
Victoria
MAS SABROSA
QUE NUNCA

RIGHT: The devastating
effect of a Flying
Clothesline

cover the sport were *El Halcón, Box y Lucha, Guerreros del Ring,* and *Lucha Libre.* These were the most respected Lucha Libre magazines and they've covered Lucha in all aspects. *From Parts Unknown* was a great magazine that was in English so the non-Latino fans could follow the Lucha world directly. With the advent of the Internet, all of this info can now be had, even for the non-Spanish speaking among us.

For years much of the information pertaining to Lucha Libre was thought lost. Recollections of matches and Luchadores, events, records, arena attendance, etc. seemed to be forever faded from our collective memory. But every so often something new pops up, a piece of information or an unknown fact recently discovered that sheds new light into a past that should not sit quietly dim in the back of people's minds. Whatever tidbits are out there, whatever few crumbs Lucha fans can dine on to sustain them until the next excavation of history is unearthed, we gladly hold on to. Once you're hooked on this sport it becomes a colorful masked addiction. You look forward to anticipate, almost crave the next live match.

With most sports today, the demarcation line between spectator and athlete is an inaccessible chasm between fan and competitor. In Lucha Libre, the wrestlers will happily talk to you after the matches, or sign an autograph or have a photo taken with you. Luchadores know what many other spoiled athletes don't understand or don't care to learn about: Without the fans there is no business.

Lucha as a Force to Reckon with Outside the Ring

Heroes and villains have always worn masks, and although Lucha Libre did not invent the concept of hiding one's true identity, it has kept the secretive tradition alive and well for over eighty years. Fictional characters like Zorro, the Scarlet Pimpernel, the Spirit and the Lone Ranger have always done virtuous deeds without the heavy burden of public notoriety to hamper their true motivations. Villains have always worn masks to hide their true nature, to keep their dark side hidden away from the glaring light of righteousness, whether it was a make-believe figure like the French turn-of-the-century arch fiend Fantômas or the chainsaw–wielding cannibalistic lunatic "Leatherface" from *The Texas Chainsaw Massacre*.

Keeping one's true nature hidden, for good or evil purposes, is essential if one is to be totally dedicated to the task at hand. Whether it be heroic or treacherous, anonymity is the key factor to keeping one's morality in balance. Could Joe Average actually have an ultra altruistic alter ego and perform for people without the spotlight of celebrity in his eyes, blinding his noble aspirations, if he wasn't concealed? This hypothetical happened in, of all places, the country that still respects the masked man of virtue: Mexico.

ABOVE: Último Dragón delivering a Flying Drop Kick

Enter SuperBarrio, a masked political candidate who came out of a splinter group of the PRI (Partido Revolucionario Insitucional) in the mid-eighties. SuperBarrio became the leader of a group that challenged the right-wing Partido de Accion National's inability to respond to the needs of the indigent, poor and misplaced of the country. In many ways this politico enmascarado was a modern-day Robin Hood, fighting for the downtrodden and despondent. Just as Lucha fans looked up to El Santo years earlier in his fight against vampire women and Martian invaders, the poor of Mexico looked to SuperBarrio as a savior against their perceived tormentors, the unsympathetic powers in charge. He carried the belief with him that all good Luchadores will triumph over corruption. The idea of a masked hero fighting for social justice didn't stop with SuperBarrio.

Soon other like-minded men on missions of mercy started to pop up and champion the causes of the underprivileged, the environment, animals, and for gay rights.

Soon after SuperBarrio's debut into the political arena there came Ecologista Universal, who was on a mission to stop the Laguna Verde nuclear reactor. Superanimal fought for animal rights. Mujer Maravilla fought for women's rights. Supernino fought for homeless children, and SuperGay lobbied for the rights of gays and lesbians. It seems that for almost every political platform there was someone ready to put on the mask and go to bat for a cause. Fray Tormenta (Friar Storm), dramatized in *Nacho Libre*, took to wearing a mask and performing as an enmascarado in the evening, while still attending to his daily duties as a priest. It seemed the good father wrestled for years in order to bring money into his poor parish, and he even started to perform his masses in front of his congregation wearing his colorful masks.

The idea of justice coming from the ranks of their own is something that has always been within the Mexican people, from the revolutionary spirit of Emilio Zapata and Pancho Villa to the brave exploits of El Santo and Blue Demon to the heroic character of Fray Tormenta and SuperBarrio. The Mexican people have expected no less than a champion to rise out of their despair and lead them to whatever victory they are fighting for.

The influence of Lucha Libre around the world is strong, from its recent political momentum behind social causes to current art movements. Lucha Libre has a distinct flair and style uniquely unto itself. No other culture has been affected by Lucha the way Japan has. In the next chapter, former WWE writer and former professor of film studies at the George Washington University Ranjan Chhibber, PhD, contributes his expertise on how Mexican Lucha Libre influenced the current Japanese style of professional wrestling, puroresu. Japanese pro wrestling is gathering momentum all throughout Asia but also in the United States. Soon both Japanese pro wrestling and Lucha Libre will have strongholds and huge fan followings in North America.

THE OFTEN UNTOLD TALE OF LUCHA COMICS

by Keith J. Rainville

Mexi-movie superheroes like El Santo may be familiar, but the unsung hero of the prolific Lucha film genre can be said to have been comic book publisher Jose G. Cruz.

In the 1940s, Cruz was a pioneer in the "fotomontage" publishing technique. Comics were constructed from posed model photos composited with painted backgrounds, illustrated "special effects" and hand-lettered word balloons. These "fumetti" comics were cheap to produce and could be turned around factory-style with amazing speed.

Enter Santo, who in 1951 debuted as a pulp hero. All the groundwork of the Mexican masked wrestler superhero idiom was laid here—the relationship with law enforcement, desperate victims pleading for the wrestler's help in the locker room post-match, scientists in trouble, damsels in distress, kid sidekicks, femme fatales. Signature vehicles like sporty convertibles, motorbikes and jetpacks, the secret hideout full of gadgets . . . all things most consider convention of the film genre but were actually cribbed from the comics.

Film studios may have caught up to Cruz quickly, but what they never had was the freedom that the photomontage format offered. Imagination was the limit. Santo fought giant squids, towering swamp monsters, flying

OPPOSITE: A cover from José G. Cruz's highly collectable and very rare Santo comics

BELOW: Rafael Navarro's cool Lucha-inspired character *Masks of Sonámbulo*: worth checking out and collecting

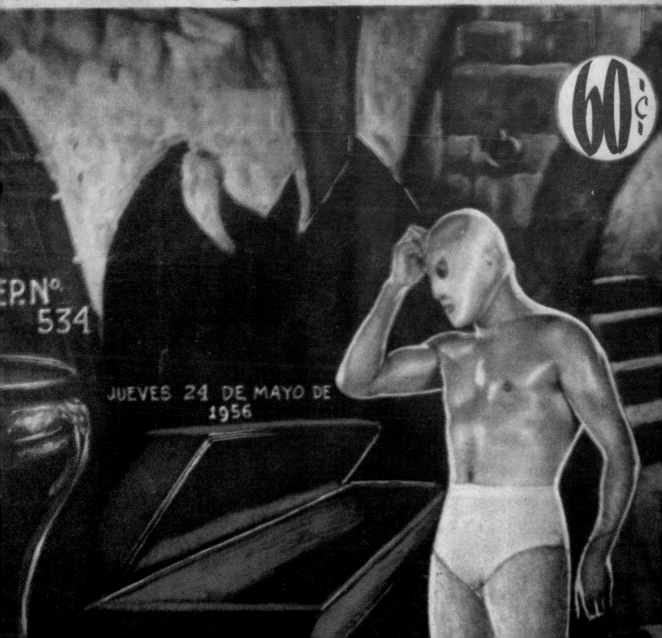

EL INCREIBLE

13

Blue Demon

COLOMBIA $7
ECUADOR S/7
VENEZUELA 1.50 BS.

ESTRELLA INVITADA

MALENA
DORIA

batmen, insectoid aliens and more. He was shrunk to a tiny
size, battled rats with sewing needles, and was assaulted by
vengeful Lilliputian pygmies. The films, with their modest, at
best, budgets, could hardly compete with the over-the-top su-
perheroics of the comic book Santo.

So popular was the book format, it ran for three decades,
selling over half a million copies per issue at its height, and
at one point published three times a week! To get an idea of
just how much of an institution the Santo comics were, consider that Mexicans read their comics. They don't seal them
in Lucite to ensure their collectibility. Furthermore, the books
are passed around from brother to
brother, sister to sister, with dad
and grandma thrown in to boot.
Then, you can sell them back to the
newsstand, and another family can
pick them up used. All told, a single Mexican comic probably has
over a dozen readers in its life-
span. Multiply that number times
the massive print runs, and you
get a notion of just how omni-
present these pulp adventures
were in Mexico.

That prolific readership,
however, has a drawback.
The books just didn't survive,
and there are precious few
vintage collections now. As
the original art was pulled
apart and recycled for latter
use, there is little hope for
quality reprints, either. The
comics may have been the
single biggest chapter in
the formation of the Lucha-
superhero genre, but at
this point they are on their
way to becoming lost. 💀

OPPOSITE: **Not to be
outdone by Santo, Blue
Demon got into the
comic book act as well**

BELOW: **If you come
across any of the Lucha
comics, grab 'em as
fast as you can—there
are not that many left,
so their value by fans
increases each year**

11

Lucharesu:

The International Impact of Lucha Libre Wrestling

BY RANJAN CHHIBBER, PhD

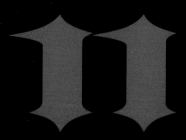

THE HISTORY OF *Lucha Libre wrestling is not something that is a uniquely Mexican phenomenon; nor is it an entertainment form confined to Spanish-speaking diasporas around the world. The mark of a true cultural phenomenon lies in its international impact. While Mil Máscaras is an icon that has transcended Lucha Libre, appearing in films and TV shows that have nothing to do with wrestling, the real test is whether Lucha Libre as a style and wrestling form has made a mark around the world.*

OPPOSITE: An audacious aerial assault ABOVE: Wearing the crimson mask

Its biggest impact on wrestling has not been in the United States but, rather, in the East, specifically, Japan. Many Japanese wrestlers have made their way to Mexico to relearn how to wrestle, to pick up a new style, and to fashion a new identity that turns them from unknown jobbers to main event players. Mexico, not America, is considered to be the Mecca of professional wrestling for the majority of Japanese wrestlers.

The wrestling styles of Japan and Mexico could not be more different: The high-flying Lucha Libre style is not usually found in Japanese wrestling (puroresu), which favors a hard-core, bloody wrestling, and fans prefer submission endings over Lucha Libre's high-spot finishes. But like any other country's wrestling entertainment industry, variety is necessary to sustain viewer interest. In America, for the majority of Hulk Hogans in the ring, there need to be a few Rey Mysterios to provide diversity; similarly, Japan has turned to Mexico for diversity.

Japanese promoters decided to import a few Mexican stars to add this necessary spice to its promotions. While many puroresu athletes are known for being very serious and without any flair at all to their personalities, the Lucha Libre stars are known for their flamboyance, their colorful costumes, and, most importantly, their masks. Masked wrestlers were very rare in Japan prior to the hiring of Lucha Libre stars, and this fascinated Japanese audiences more than anything else. The ubiquitous Mil Máscaras became an icon in Japan (as he did in every other country he appeared in).

The Difficult Birth of the Japanese Pro Wrestler

When puroresu athletes saw the reception Japanese fans gave to Lucha Libre stars visiting their own home turf, many of them decided that imitation was the sincerest form of flattery . . . and the masked Japanese wrestler was born.

However, his birth was not easy. His first problem was that the mask was divorced from the cultural significance that it holds in Mexico. For Japanese fans, the mask was at best a novelty that provided an interesting diversion from the traditional Japanese wrestler. The mask was used by mainly foreign wrestlers. For example, the American masked wrestler Dick Beyer, better known as the Destroyer. The mask was so associated with the Destroyer that when he took off his mask decades later at a press conference to talk to fans, they were appalled and offended. The Destroyer and Mil Máscaras became the foreign fixtures of All Japan Pro Wrestling in the '70s. The point is, however, that they are American and Mexican, respectively. There is still no indigenous masked wrestler in Japan of renown at this point in time.

Japanese wrestlers in makeup were the closest thing to masked wrestlers in puroresu. Wrestlers like the Great Kabuki in the late '70s and early '80s personified the most colorful of indigenous Japanese wrestlers, thanks to his excessive face paint. In Japanese culture, makeup holds the same traditional significance that the mask does in Mexico; it is used in religious rituals and theatrical forms.

In Japanese wrestling, the Kabuki-influenced wrestler was able to portray a rare persona that was denied to the majority of his puroresu compatriots. The Japanese wrestler with makeup, therefore, had tradition to fall back on; the masked wrestler in Japan had no easy cultural antecedent to fall back upon.

While the lack of a masked tradition was one impediment to Japanese wrestlers appearing with them on, the other difficulty they faced was puroresu's reliance on hard-core violence and submission wrestling. The aerial Luchador style was all but unknown to them, with no puroresu dojo able to teach it.

The first Japanese wrestler to learn the Lucha Libre style of wrestling was Hiroaki Hamada of New Japan Pro Wrestling. Hamada was a talented wrestler, but was held back due to his very short stature:

5'6", which was short even by Japanese standards. Rather than face a life being a perennial jobber, Hamada left for Mexico in the late '70s to try his luck there. Joining Mexico's Universal Wrestling Association, he achieved an unprecedented level of success there for a foreign competitor. They gave him the name "El Gran Hamada," and he outperformed his own Lucha Libre teachers in terms of his acrobatic artistry. When he returned to Japan, he brought this new style of wrestling back with him, and audiences were delighted.

Never had they seen one of their own wrestlers use such death-defying moves. El Gran Hamada continued to wrestle with his Spanish name as well, thus defying another Japanese wrestling tradition (using Japanese or American names). Rejuvenated by his Mexican wrestling conversion, he went from being a disrespected jobber to main eventer in the '80s in Japan. He was so successful, he opened his own promotion in Japan called Universal Lucha Libre, where he trained many young aspiring Japanese wrestlers in this Mexican style. One of the reasons he did so was that it was becoming increasingly difficult for him to put together coherent matches with his more traditional Japanese wrestling opponents, the latter of whom found it difficult to adapt to his style.

The legendary Japanese wrestler and booker Antonio Inoki decided to have some of his wrestlers train in Mexico as well. Inoki's top young student of the '70s, Tatsumi "The Dragon" Fujinami, was short and undersized, and Inoki did not want him being overshadowed by the bigger wrestlers around him. He sent Fujinami to Mexico to train with wrestlers of a similar body type, and when he returned to Japan, Inoki used Fujinami's talents to create a cruiserweight division. Fujinami makes famous around the world his newly learned style, moves such as "The Dragon Sleeper" and "The Dragon Suplex," but it should be remembered that these moves were developed in Mexico, not Japan. It is also significant that Inoki could find no local Japanese talent to showcase Fujinami's style in the '70s: He has to import Mexican Luchadores to use as enhancement talent. Fujinami wouldn't be his only student who made it big, thanks to Mexico.

The 1980s: Decade of the Tiger Mask

Satoru Sayama grew up as a big fan of Antonio Inoki, but as part of a younger generation in Japan, he was also exposed to Mil Máscaras. Sayama is a perfect example of just how much Máscaras had permeated Japanese culture. In an interview with *The Weekly Gong*, in Japan, he says, "When I was in eighth grade, I wore a mask that I designed for an event during a school festival. . . . I designed it after Máscaras. The reason I started wrestling was Inoki-san, but Mil Máscaras was always on my mind."

What further differentiates Sayama is that he was already a wrestling star prior to adopting his masked gimmick. He wrestled under his own name in the late '70s. His wrestling style was clearly influenced by Lucha Libre, but his persona was not that of the masked Mexican superstars he adored.

Ignoring the saying "if it ain't broke, don't fix it," Inoki decided to repackage Sayama in the early '80s with a masked gimmick called "Tiger Mask." Tiger Mask was already known in Japan as a manga (comic book) superhero. In the manga, he was a wrestling superhero who battled villains using Lucha Libre moves. Inoki correctly predicted that making this manga superhero a real-life wrestler would make his promotion lots of money. Sayama's training in Mexico made him the only one who could perfectly bring Tiger Mask to life.

As Tiger Mask, Sayama became the biggest draw in Japan for at least three years in the early '80s. One of his biggest feuds during that time was with the legendary British wrestler Tom Billington, otherwise known as the Dynamite Kid. As the maskless Sayama, his feud with the Dynamite Kid would have been just as good, but the growing fascination with Mexican-style masked wrestlers in Japan took these tremendous matches and transformed them into

OPPOSITE: Shamu with a leg (or fin) up on Chilango

mythological manga-style battles. What is injected into Sayama is personality, and this personality injected a larger-than-life electricity to the matches.

Japanese wrestlers everywhere took notice of the success of Tiger Mask. Even if one was already a famous wrestler, and even if he had trained in Mexico, it was a mask that led to the big money. Moreover, the mask itself could now be said to have its roots in a uniquely Japanese tradition: a manga superhero. The link between masks and wrestlers so inherent in Mexican culture was starting to take root in Japan, thanks to the success of Tiger Mask. Arguably, like in Mexico, Tiger Mask became greater than the wrestler: When Sayama took a few sabbaticals from the ring, there were at least three other wrestlers who adopted the Tiger Mask gimmick.

Lucha Libre's influence on Japan cannot be understated. The lives of the Japanese men who wrestled in Mexico are a small part of the transformation that has occurred in Japanese society thanks to Mexican wrestling. No less than five promotions in Japan have been devoted almost exclusively to Lucharesu, some with a great deal of success. Opening up doors for smaller-statured Japanese men everywhere, these promotions breathed a new life into the stale versions of Japanese puroresu.

The Great Sasuke himself has transcended his status as a Lucharesu. He was elected to a state government position on April 13, 2003, making him the first masked wrestler to be elected to high office. Sasuke refuses to remove his mask in the legislature, no doubt honoring the Lucha Libre tradition of always appearing with one's mask on. The Japanese media focused upon the Mexican roots of this desire, providing its society with insight into that culture.

Mexico should be proud of instituting a lasting change not only in Japanese wrestling, but in its popular culture and now its politics. Japan has opened its arms to this facet of Mexican culture, and happily allows it to breed. The etymology of the word "Lucharesu" itself shows just how multicultural Japanese wrestling has become: the Japanese word *puroresu* was a Japanese version of the American words "pro wrestling"; the addition of the Spanish word "Lucha" shows how Japanese wrestling, language and culture is evolving still.

12

The End of the Book and the Spread of Lucha

SO THIS IS *the end of the journey that I started so long ago. Well, actually it's the end of the book; the story and journey of Lucha Libre still continue. I wanted to say once again that I would not have made it this far without the help of some pretty special friends and some wonderful new ones I made during the course of putting this book together. What I attempted to do was to give you a taste of what Lucha Libre is all about, a little history about the sport, a little background on the movies, some insight into the lives of the men who made it what is was and is today. Hopefully that small taste whet your appetite and you will seek out the world of Lucha on your own.*

I feel like I should say something funny here or at least attempt

OPPOSITE: Masked, Izod-wearing, *cerveza*-drinking fans at a Lucha show ABOVE: A sexy Luchadora from Andrew Barr's awesome series, "Something a Go-Go"

my own stab at humor and leave you readers with a smile, but I wanted to express something about the people I have met and become close with in the course of doing this book. Almost everyone who helped me with this project couldn't have been nicer and more giving of their time and effort, and in some cases I was a total stranger coming into their lives, asking for favors. These people are the reflection of what Lucha Libre really is, a fraternity of friends, an extended family of fans. I still get a warm feeling when I walk into one of the many venues I have covered and some of the people there know me, and even if we don't speak the same language, that warm smile or friendly nod says volumes on who these people, the fans, really are. The men who step in the ring are the heart of Lucha Libre, but it is the fans who are the soul, and together they have created a living, breathing, bleeding, sweating, loving, heroic universe where the sun is a square mat-covered ring and the cosmos are the legends and spectators who have come before and who will arrive in the future.

Finally, I wanted to leave you with this; it is a good indicator of the types of people who have come out of the Lucha Libre world. When I was at the end of my work in pro wrestling I was going through a pretty rough time. Actually it was one of the worst weeks of my life. It was one of those times when you get bad news on Monday and think, "Well, the week's shot already," then you get that call on Wednesday that makes Monday's call look like a walk in the park and now you're like, "What the hell? What voodoo gods did I piss off to get screwed like this?" Then you get that call on Friday and as soon as you hear the phone ring, your skin starts to crawl, and after that conversation you're about to find a railroad track so you can lay your head down and wait for the 5:15 to come and put you out of your misery. That is exactly how I felt my last week on the road. I received three devastating phone calls on the personal level and they sucker-punched me numb. Without sounding maudlin, it was everything from someone dying to someone soon to be dying, real pleasant dinner conversation, and to make matters worse I couldn't get home in time because I found myself headed to England to do an international show.

Now I was feeling real down in the dumps, substrata miserable, and all I wanted to do was finish the shows and get to the states and my wife as soon as possible. After the last show was done, I decided the quickest way for me to get stateside was to jump on the charter with the wrestler, and I'd be home in five hours. At least I'd reach the trouble that awaited me before the next day, but guess what? That wouldn't happen. Once again the gods that play with us mere mortals for enjoyment decided to pull the rug from underneath me. The charter plane that I got myself on to so I could get home faster was delayed a day and a half because of a broken something or other. I couldn't believe it. The one time I had to be home on time and I was stuck in an airport hotel until five o'clock in the morning, trying to drown my sorrows in Jack Daniels.

As I was on my second round of self-pity Eddie Guerrero walked in. He came over to me and told me he knew of my predicament. He asked me how my wife was doing. I said as well as she could be. Then he looked me in the eye and said, "How are you doing, Dan?" I gave the ol' cavalier smile and said everything was all right. Then he gently placed his hand on my shoulder and warmly stared at me and asked again, "Dan . . . how are you doing?" I told him that I had seen better days. Then he told me, with the most heartfelt sincerity I have ever heard one person convey to another, "Man, I know it is rough, but I am here for you if you need anything at all. Remember Jesus loves you . . . and so do I, bro." Then he gave me a hug and left. The next week, my last days on the job, I saw Eddie walking up the back of the arena. He saw me and smiled and hurried over to me. The first thing out of his mouth was, "Hey, how is your wife doing? I've been thinking about the both of you all week, and you have been in my prayers." He quoted some scripture to me and once again confessed his love for me, just as one brother would to another. It was genuine and warm and comforting. Here was a guy who was the biggest draw in the wrestling business; he had a thousand things on his mind, his matches and his family. He was in pain a lot of the time backstage because of the bumps he took over the years in the ring. And the first thing on his mind and out of his mouth when he saw me was how my wife and I were doing. Eddie was a born-again Christian; he walked the walk and talked the talk. He didn't say things he didn't mean and he told you exactly how he felt. He loved God, he loved the wrestling business, he loved his fans and most of all he loved his family, his mother, his brothers and sisters, his dad, his nephew Chavo Jr. and especially his lovely wife and his three daughters. When he talked to you, he spoke *to* you, not *at* you. He didn't just listen to what you had to say; he heard the words you were speaking. In his eyes was the purest sense of honesty that I had ever seen in any human being. If a person is defined by his actions and character, than no man had more character and honor than Eddie Guerrero. I would marvel at how in a minute before he went out to perform, he would be stiff and sore all over, but the second he stepped past those curtains and heard the roar of the fans, every ache and pain vanished and he was there to give the crowd every ounce of blood, sweat and tears he had in his proud body. Eddie didn't just raise the bar; he kicked it out of orbit.

I contacted Eddie about doing this project and including his dad, Gory, and his family in the book; he was very excited to be a part of it. He called me one day and I didn't hear the phone, one of those moments I will always regret. He left a message saying that he was happy to partake in this endeavor I was undertaking to bring Lucha Libre to the fans. He asked me how my wife was and how I was. He told me he was thinking of me and to take care of myself. The last thing he ever said to me before he hung up was, "God bless."

A little time later my friend Michael Cole, the wrestling announcer, called me up. He knew that I liked Eddie and he wanted me to hear the bad news first. He told me that Eddie had passed away the night before in his hotel room. I don't know if you would call it shock; it was something more, a numbness shot all the way through my body and into my heart. A profound sadness came over me as the day went on and the realization slowly started to set in that I would never speak to my friend again, that the fans would never be able to watch him perform again, that his family would not be able to hold and hug him again in this life. My eyes still water as I write these words several months later. Eddie was what Lucha Libre was all about, honesty, integrity, loyalty, friendship and honor. They called Eddie "Latino Heat" and his name and legend will burn warmly in the hearts of the millions that loved him. There will never be another.

REST IN PEACE.

ACKNOWLEDGMENTS

In other words a heartfelt thanks to all the people who, without their help, this book would not have been made.

To Gasaprin, for his kindness and expertise and love for Lucha.

To Juan Guerrero, a masterful artisan and a man with the patience of a saint (or a Santo).

To Cassandro, a shining jewel in the world of Lucha, an *exótico* extraordinaire and performer nonpareil.

To Eric Cadien, owner of the famous Hollywood Book & Poster shop, whose diligent excavating in the mountainous memorabilia collection that is his store unearthed so many incredible images for this book.

To Tim Sims, whose artistic vision and guidance and friendship helped relieve some of the strain of this project.

To Daniel Chavira, who not only donated his incredible portfolio but also his family's rich history in Lucha Libre.

To Leo Solis, who patiently took me through his astonishing collection of Lucha memorabilia and donated many images he has collected throughout the years.

To Antonio Pelayo, a good friend and talented artist, who did the incredible El Santo drawing just for this book.

To Ranjan Chhibber, whose friendship, support, and loyalty were only matched by his knowledge and love for wrestling.

To Brian Moran and his wonderful *Santo Street*, a truly incredible fanzine that is full of amazing interviews, facts and reviews of this genre.

To Keith (The Man with a Thousand Titles) Rainville, who is THE expert on Lucha, for sharing his insight and expertise with me.

To Eddie Mort, the genius behind "Mucha Lucha," who gave me so many wonderful images that it was painful to pick out only a few.

To Marvin Miranda, for his storytelling knowledge and bilingual assistance (and record collection).

To Raúl Cruz, for his help and access to his great website and Lucha Libre forum that he runs.

To Dorothy Lee, a godsend and gifted artist.

To my brother Eric, for his computer skills (he was born with technical savvy and I got all the good looks).

Special thanks to the following contributors:

David Schow

Victor Llamas

Lucha VaVoom

Danny Amis of Los Straightjackets

And to Steve Cattani, a friend and advocate, who carried on the good fight. Rest in Peace.

But most of all, to my photographer and cohort in crime in this endeavor, Edward McGinty, who put himself in harm's way many times to get the shot I was screaming for. Without his talent none of this would have been possible.